STRENGTHENING DEMOCRACY

Strengthening Democracy

A Parliamentary Perspective

RON GOULD
CHRISTINE JACKSON
LOREN WELLS

Dartmouth
Aldershot • Brookfield USA • Singapore • Sydney

Published by
Dartmouth Publishing Company Limited
Gower House
Croft Road
Aldershot
Hants GU11 3HR
England

Dartmouth Publishing Company
Old Post Road
Brookfield
Vermont 05036
USA

Written for and published in
association with the
Commonwealth Parliamentary Association
Suite 700, Westminster House
7 Millbank
London SW1P 3JA
United Kingdom

A CIP catalogue record for this book is available from the British Library.

ISBN 1 85521 775 9

Typeset by Manton Typesetters, 5–7 Eastfield Road, Louth, Lincolnshire, United Kingdom.

Printed and bound in Great Britain by Ipswich Book Co. Ltd., Ipswich, Suffolk

Contents

1 Introduction

In late January and early February 1994, a conference on *Strengthening Democracy Throughout the World: Electoral Systems, Election Monitoring and Good Government* was held at Wiston House in the United Kingdom. The Conference was attended by a distinguished group of representatives from Commonwealth countries, the European Union, the United States, and other countries, as well as from the United Nations. Presentations were wide-ranging and covered subjects related to the strengthening of democracy. A list of those in attendance and the conference agenda can be found as Appendices 2 and 3 at the end of this volume.

The Commonwealth Parliamentary Association advised that many of the ideas and views presented, not only in the plenary sessions, but also in the discussion groups, would be useful for the information and guidance of Parliamentarians generally. It recommended that these be identified and combined with other applicable views and theories in a document which would reflect the main themes of the Conference. What follows is an attempt to achieve this objective – to present a parliamentary perspective on some aspects of strengthening democracy throughout the world. It will be evident that this document, like the Conference, focuses on a selected series of subjects, and therefore does not claim to discuss all of the initiatives which could be considered as essential to strengthening democracy. Nor does it purport to deal exhaustively with every aspect of election observation or monitoring. However, it does reflect many of the views, comments and suggestions put forward by individuals who have extensive experience in attempts to strengthen democracy in various countries in the world. It should therefore provide useful reference material for future democratic development initiatives.

In conjunction with the Conference and this report, the Commonwealth Parliamentary Association also undertook to have *A Guide for Election Observers* prepared. This document can be found as Appendix 1. The Guide focuses on the observation of elections and is designed to be a comprehensive working document which takes observers from the period well before the election to the post-voting phase during which votes are actually counted and results proclaimed. As a working document, the Reference Guide contains a checklist to assist observers when visiting polling stations on voting days. The Guide also attempts to incorporate a number of the viewpoints which are expressed in the various chapters of this volume.

2 The Role of Parliamentary Associations

The role of parliamentary associations in the development and support of democracy and democratic institutions cannot be underestimated. In recent years, the membership of some of these associations has played a major role in the development and strengthening of democratic principles and institutions around the world. Many individuals have assisted with the drafting of constitutions and electoral laws, acted as election observers or monitors, and participated in seminars after an electoral event to help with the transition to a democratic government. This list of activities is by no means exhaustive, but may provide some indication of the depth of the commitment of these parliamentarians to democratic processes.

There are many benefits which result from the participation of parliamentarians in these activities. One of the major ones, however, develops from using teams or panels of individuals from different member-countries. What their participation indicates is the conviction that democracy is something which can develop within any state, reflecting the particular culture, heritage or history of that nation. This principle and this diversity are personified in the representatives of the parliamentary association.

Depending on the particular mandate of the parliamentary association and the size of its membership, the organization may focus its efforts in one particular area of endeavour. This is not to say that it will limit its involvement, only that such an approach may facilitate the most efficient use of its resources and its membership.

Although there are any number of parliamentary associations around the world, international or regional, an examination of the activities of the Commonwealth Parliamentary Association (CPA), the Inter-Parliamentary Union (IPU) and the International Assembly of French-Speaking Parliamentarians (AIPLF) should provide an indication of their involvement.

The Commonwealth Parliamentary Association

The Commonwealth Parliamentary Association works to promote parliamentary democracy and respect for democratic institutions and to foster closer understanding, cooperation and friendship between the Parliamentarians of its member branches. Membership of the CPA is dependent upon the existence of a fully-functioning and democratically-elected Parliament.

The single greatest resource of the CPA is its membership. This is comprised of all Parliamentarians – government and opposition – and does not depend on the size of the elected body. Members range from those with parliamentary knowledge acquired over decades to those whose service is measured in months, and from elected bodies manifesting many years of history to those only recently established.

Parliamentary democracy is promoted in a variety of ways by the members of the CPA. Members come together for an annual conference; parliamentary seminars are held periodically, and ideas are exchanged through various publications and newsletters. In 1985, the rules, regulations and procedures governing the conduct of elections – one of the most basic activities in parliamentary democracy – were the subject of three days of discussion by seven Commonwealth Members of Parliament at a special study group meeting held in Halifax (Nova Scotia). Held under the auspices of the CPA, this study group produced a report on the laws and practices which determine how political power is acquired and lost. A copy of this Report is attached as Appendix 5.

In October 1991, the Commonwealth Heads of Government meeting in Zimbabwe produced what is commonly known as the 'Harare Declaration'. This establishes the protection and promotion of democracy, the rule of law, just and honest government, and human rights (including equality and equal rights for women) as being priorities for members of the Commonwealth to pursue.

In recent years, therefore, the Commonwealth has been seeking to fulfil its commitment to democracy by placing new emphasis on the use of Commonwealth assets and experience in fostering democracy, good governance and human rights. It is in this context that the CPA, which was specifically referred to in the Declaration, plays a key role, sharing its skills and expertise with a wider audience than its own members.

For several years, the CPA has been furnishing the Commonwealth Secretariat with names of Commonwealth Parliamentarians who are well qualified by experience and expertise to take part in the Commonwealth's election observation missions. In addition, CPA members have been sent on specialized missions to countries to provide advice on the structure of parliamentary institutions long before elections are due. The CPA has also compiled a large body of voter education material from its members, making this available to organizations in South Africa. Since no Parliament can be said to be functioning properly if its members have not been legitimately elected, the CPA has made a useful contribution in this respect.

The CPA believes that all efforts expended to facilitate a free and fair election are wasted if they do not lead to the successful establishment of a properly functioning, democratic Parliament and government. To this end, as soon as possible after the election, the CPA provides post-election seminars for newly-elected members, familiarizing them with the mechanics of their parliamentary duties and the rules and procedures in their respective Parliaments.

While Parliaments with a long history are able to furnish their new members with the requisite training, newly-established Parliaments benefit greatly from the expertise of other CPA members. The CPA arranges national, regional and Commonwealth-wide seminars, where Speakers and other senior members provide guidance. Such seminars are especially useful for members recently elected in countries changing from military rule or from a one-party system to multi-party democracy. Topics for these seminars include: the roles, responsibilities and privileges of a Member of Parliament; party organization within parliament and the role of minority parties; the business of the House and the role of the Speaker and staff of Parliament; the committee system, and the evolution of parliamentary democracy.

The CPA facilitates the proper functioning of Parliament by assisting in the professionalization of Parliament's operatives – its elected members. The CPA is committed to meeting as many requests for assistance as possible in the firm belief that, by doing so, it is manifestly fulfilling its role to help plant and foster the seeds of democratic parliamentary government.

The Inter-Parliamentary Union

Founded in 1889, the Inter-Parliamentary Union is a world-wide organization of parliamentarians committed to establishing and developing representative institutions within their respective States and to promoting international peace and cooperation, particularly by supporting the objectives of the United Nations. Of the 164 legislative assemblies meeting in the world's sovereign states, 118 are represented in the IPU. Each of these legislative assemblies establishes a National Group, usually formed by the Parliament as a whole. Delegates to the IPU are normally drawn from all political parties and act as individual parliamentarians rather than on behalf of their respective governments. Parliamentarians of different countries and ideologies are thus brought together to study and debate cultural, economic, political and social problems of international significance.

Of prime importance to the IPU is the ability of parliamentarians to function freely and efficiently. Through its programme for the Study and

Promotion of Representative Institutions, the IPU gathers and disseminates information on the constitutional powers, structures and working methods of national parliaments, on the status of their members, on electoral systems, and on parliamentary elections and their results. The Union also publishes comparative studies on parliaments and electoral systems, periodicals, monographs, and reference material for use by parliamentarians, academics and the general public.

In 1973, the IPU launched a Technical Cooperation Programme to mobilize support and funding for the parliaments of new and developing countries. Supported by the United Nations Development Programme (UNDP), and bilateral donors, the Programme offers expert advice on the structure and working methods of legislative assemblies, as well as on the organization of staff training courses and on technical equipment and other resources. The technical cooperation activities undertaken by the Union involve the following: advising parliaments on their role, structure and working methods (based on a comparative knowledge of the functioning of different parliamentary systems), assessing the needs of parliaments in relation to the training of parliamentary staff and the provision of material resources and technical equipment (including advice in relation to building, enlarging or providing equipment for premises suited to the requirements of parliamentary activities), as well as elaborating and implementing technical cooperation projects.

The IPU has periodically organized international symposia for parliamentarians, senior parliamentary officials and civil servants, scholars and experts, in order to study the functioning of parliamentary institutions. It also offers yearly information seminars on all aspects of IPU activities.

The Union cooperates closely with the UN and its agencies and also maintains relations with other inter-governmental and regional associations and other inter-parliamentary organizations.

The International Assembly of French-Speaking Parliamentarians

The International Assembly of French-Speaking Parliamentarians (AIPLF) was created in 1967 and now has 45 member parliaments from five continents. Its main objectives are to act as a democratic link between French-speaking institutions and peoples, to encourage cooperation and reinforce unity within the French-speaking world, and to promote democracy, the state of law and human rights.

The AIPLF now has an important role to play in a number of projects designed to promote democracy which have emanated from within its member-countries. The Assembly has also obtained the collaboration of the

Heads of State and Government for each one of its actions aimed at supporting the democratic process and at establishing and consoliding parliamentary institutions in French-speaking countries.

There are three main areas of involvement to achieve this end. The Assembly has introduced a programme to support documentary services in parliaments of the South which, in the initial phase, will either create or consolidate the documentary services of the parliaments of five African countries. The Assembly organizes discussion and information seminars for Members of Parliament, and practical training and proficiency courses for parliamentary civil servants. The themes of discussion include the organization of government, the administration of justice, the electoral system, the financing of political parties, the progression of bills, etc.

In addition, the participation of the Assembly in election monitoring missions is of growing importance. The Assembly is especially concerned with the period following these missions, with a particular focus on supporting the creation of new parliamentary assemblies. In light of its own experience and similar conclusions reached by other organizations that participate in electoral missions, the AIPLF is planning to go much further in future. It is felt, therefore, that to truly contribute to the democratization process, the election monitoring missions should ideally be preceded by technical assistance on constitutional and legislative writing and, whenever possible, should also include technical (and in many cases material) support for the organization of the election.

Furthermore, the Assembly considers it desirable to help put into place the technical and administrative services for newly-elected parliamentary assemblies and also to assist the harmonious integration of these assemblies with the political and social institutions of the countries concerned.

The Assembly considers that it should also organize seminars for newly-elected parliamentarians in countries where election monitoring missions have taken place. These seminars may even be made mandatory and become part of a truly integrated programme to aid the democratization process, including support measures at all three stages – pre-electoral, electoral and post-electoral.

While describing these initiatives to support the democratization process, the Assembly underlines the specific contribution of its members, the parliamentarians. Parliamentarians have the necessary experience related to this field of endeavour, be it for the organization and holding of elections or for the establishment of viable parliamentary institutions.

Conclusion

With the concerns and activities of the Commonwealth Parliamentary Association, the Inter-Parliamentary Union and the International Association of French-Speaking Parliamentarians being very similar, it is essential that these organizations not only use their own resources wisely but also avoid duplicating each other's efforts.

It has become evident that there are demands being placed not only on the above-mentioned organizations, but on many others as well. It may be necessary to encourage further collaboration and cooperation among organizations, be they governmental or non-governmental, in order that they may share resources and, if possible, become further involved in elements of the democratization process. In this way, all may come to play increasingly constructive roles.

3 Overview: The Importance of Free and Fair Elections to Good Governance (based on papers presented by Sir Anthony Siaguru and the Hon Clive Griffiths)

'... the promotion of democracy and good governance requires a participatory civic culture based on tolerance and mutual respect and a corresponding legal and institutional framework to safeguard and advance core human values.'
Sir Anthony Siaguru, from his opening address to the *Conference on Strengthening Democracy*, 31 January 1994, Wiston House, UK.

'There are several criteria by which to assess the nature of a political regime calling itself a "democracy". First, one can ask whether the elections of representatives are free. Second, is it the case that these elections provide an effective choice for the electors? Third, does the body of elected representatives have effective power and control of the state apparatus? Fourth, do there exist the basic freedoms necessary for a citizen to participate in the democratic process? ... The extent to which many of the ... attributes of democracy are made real depends on the existence of an independent judiciary and courts to which everyone can have access.'
J. Patrick Boyer in *Political Rights: the Legal Framework of Elections in Canada* (1981).

'Elections are the lifeblood of any democracy ... [but] what is a free and fair election? The acid test must surely be whether [the election] produces a government truly representative of the people's will. ... The most technically successful "free and fair" election will be totally wasted if it does not lead to the successful establishment of a properly functioning democratic parliament and government.'
The Hon Clive Griffiths, MLC in his address to the *Conference on Strengthening Democracy*, 31 January 1994, Wiston House, UK.

Context

In the early months of 1994, democracy in some form or other was front and centre in the thoughts of citizens around the world. Amongst the issues on our minds were the following: the anxious wait for the first truly democratic elections in South African history to be held; the abrogation of basic human rights taking place during so-called 'ethnic cleansing' and war in the former Yugoslavia; the first democratic vote by Ukrainians since 1917, held in a climate of rapidly advancing social and economic decay; and the desperation in Haiti, watched from abroad by its first democratically-elected president in 187 years, as the euphoria of the elections of 1990–91 receded from memory and his country descended even further into poverty, butchery and chaos.

At the same time, at the peaceful Wiston House in West Sussex, England, democracy was much on the minds of the delegates participating in the *Conference on Strengthening Democracy Throughout the World: Electoral Systems, Election Monitoring and Good Governance*, who unanimously agreed that 'free and fair' elections are not and can never be the sole essence of the democratization process; nor can they, in and of themselves, lead to good government.

The Politics of Inclusion

The democratization movement of the current decade will undoubtedly be recorded by historians as the defining phenomenon of our times. While there can be no simplistic explanation of its origins, it must stem in large part from one overwhelming imperative – *the politics of inclusion* – which may be defined as the demand by people at the grassroots level to participate in decision making and the desire by citizens to have a say in shaping their society, its laws and governing institutions – changing, where necessary, the very fabric of life. In short, it is the expression of a fundamental desire by people to be the true authors of their individual and collective destinies. Inherent in the concept is the dynamic relationship between democracy and good governance – that creative partnership between rulers and ruled which finds expression in a freely-elected and genuinely representative government.

Fundamental Political Values in the Commonwealth

The politics of inclusion are in fact an integral element in the fundamental political values of the Commonwealth. These found expression in the 'Harare Commonwealth Declaration' of 1991 as:

- democracy
- democratic processes and institutions
- human rights in all aspects
- the rule of law and
- just and honest government.

These values underscore the multi-dimensional nature of democracy: that it is a process of dynamic interdependence between the institutions of the state and civil society, between electors and the elected, a process in which free and fair elections obviously play an essential part.

The Commonwealth Approach to Supporting the Democratic Process

In carrying out its activities to buttress democracy, the Commonwealth has sought to adopt an integrated approach, not simply in monitoring elections, but in helping to strengthen key institutions such as parliaments, judiciaries and electoral agencies in order to sustain democracy and civil society. There is a strong underlying recognition that democratic structures cannot be imposed from outside; rather they must be sustained from within. Also that the development of an indigenous democratic culture is a crucial part of the process.

Pre-Electoral Assistance

In its pre-electoral monitoring activities, the Commonwealth Secretariat's primary aim is to facilitate the creation of the most level 'playing field' possible, the essential attributes of which include the following:

- an acceptable constitution and electoral laws;
- making a separation between government and party in a one-party state and reducing unfair domination by any one person or faction;
- an independent, professional and credible electoral commission;
- access by opposition parties to the state-owned media;
- a transparent process by which a credible voter register is established;
- non-interference by the independent media, and
- an environment permitting both free expression and freedom of assembly and association.

As demonstrated in the cases of Kenya, Guyana, Ghana and Lesotho, experience has shown that *confidence building* is of central importance to the democratic process, particularly in the lead-up to an election. Early engagement with the inviting country is therefore vital to a credible and meaningful operation.

Election Observation

While the Commonwealth has neither the mandate nor the capacity to *supervise* elections, it does provide election observer groups on request from the country involved. Since 1991, those groups have been operating very successfully under guidelines laid down by the Heads of Government at the Harare Conference.

The basic approach is to send highly experienced professionals as observers into a representative sampling of polling places (after consultation with the political parties, election officials and other interested groups), rather than to attempt blanket coverage of an election.

Post-Election Assistance and Consolidation

Post-election assistance and consolidation, however, have become an increasing focus of activity for the Commonwealth Secretariat. It is thus attempting to broaden the foundations of democracy by providing technical assistance for constitutional reform, strengthening electoral commissions, reviewing election laws and upgrading electoral systems. At the same time, a wide range of seminars, workshops and conferences are being sponsored, designed to promote a democratic ethos and good governance.

In nascent democracies in particular, Commonwealth assistance has turned increasingly towards the development of national institutions, including human rights machinery; the promotion of 'civil society' in general; fostering a culture of multi-party democracy, including such concepts as a 'loyal opposition', and the development of an efficient administration. In this way, the Secretariat has been able to help member states (as well as a non-member state like Mozambique) with constitutional and electoral experts, legal drafters and other technical expertise.

Parliamentary Democracy

The Commonwealth Parliamentary Association plays a particularly vital role in developing *parliamentary democracy* through the series of conferences on parliamentary practice which it sponsors, making use as it does of its rich storehouse of parliamentary experience.

Governance and Legal Issues

As regards the broad issues of governance, the Commonwealth seeks to advance constitutional government and the rule of law by helping governments improve the quality of their legal and judicial systems in ways consistent with Commonwealth principles and practices. In light of the members-countries' shared legacy of common law, the Secretariat helps to strengthen cooperation between official agencies and legal institutions such as law reform commissions, ombudsmen, legislative drafting establishments and judiciaries. It also produces a quarterly publication, *The Commonwealth Law Bulletin*, which acts as a source of reference material on legal developments in Commonwealth countries.

As for the impact of the law on human rights, the series of judicial colloquia inaugurated in India in 1988 has continued, with three further gatherings of senior Commonwealth judges subsequently being held to consider the development of human rights jurisprudence.

Economic Environment

A favourable economic environment is vital to political stability and democratic consensus-building. The Commonwealth believes that the international promotion of democracy must be accompanied by effective cooperation of the developing country in addressing major socioeconomic problems; otherwise there exists the risk of backlash and eventual disillusionment with the democratic process by people overwhelmed by poverty and the cycle of underdevelopment. Electorates must have access to adequate resources, to jobs and to the most basic human needs. Politicians on the hustings would be well advised to guard against raising unrealistic expectations in the minds of the citizenry in this respect.

To meet the objectives identified in 1991 at Harare, the Commonwealth Secretariat has itself undergone a substantive restructuring in order to assist in the promotion of democracy, good government and development on a more cost-effective basis.

Administrative Reform

Recognizing the role of administrative reform in the overall scheme of good governance, the Secretariat is also assisting governments to review their existing structures and systems and to develop organizations which are flexible and responsive. Its activities are concentrated on re-establishing the relationship between the public, private and NGO sectors and on developing skills and managerial capacities to promote better government.

Links with Other Organizations

The Commonwealth believes in global partnership in advancing the goals of democracy; with this in mind, it has been establishing closer links with other organizations, both multilateral and bilateral, in the field of democratic development.

So What Makes an Election 'Free and Fair'?

Everyone agrees that an election must, above all, be 'free and fair', but there is no general agreement on a set of *precise* criteria against which an electoral event may be measured in this context. In fact, most believe that, when evaluating the success of an electoral process, local circumstances must be recognized and built into the assessment over and above the campaign and electoral procedures. In other words, election monitors must consider the history and culture of the society, as well as the legislative and political context of events in the pre- and post-election day periods.

Elections and election procedures should not be considered as an exact science: in *any* election one will find things which do not appear to be free and fair. For example, the rural constituencies in Western Australia contain half the voting population of their urban counterparts: some say that is not fair. When a political party loses an election, it may be tempted to blame unfair practices.

Before making a judgement on the outcome of an electoral event, therefore, the following definitions (adopted in *A Reference Guide for Election Observers*; see Appendix I) might be offered for consideration:

A 'FREE' electoral process is one where fundamental human rights and freedoms are respected, including:

- freedom of speech and expression by electors, parties, candidates and the media;
- freedom of association; that is, freedom to form organizations such as political parties and NGOs;
- freedom of assembly, to hold political rallies and to campaign;
- freedom of access to and by electors to transmit and receive political and electoral information messages;
- freedom to register as an elector, a party or a candidate;
- freedom from violence, intimidation or coercion;
- freedom of access to the polls by electors, party agents and accredited observers;
- freedom to exercise the franchise in secret, and
- freedom to question, challenge and register complaints or objections without negative repercussions.

A 'FAIR' electoral process is one where the 'playing field' is *reasonably* level and accessible to all electors, parties and candidates, and includes:

- an independent, non-partisan electoral organization to administer the process;

- guaranteed rights and protection through the constitution and electoral legislation and regulations;
- equitable representation of electors provided through the legislation;
- clearly defined universal suffrage and secrecy of the vote;
- equitable criteria and opportunities to register as an elector, a political party or a candidate;
- equitable and balanced reporting by the media;
- equitable access to financial and material resources for party and candidate campaigning;
- equitable opportunities for the electorate to receive political and voter information;
- accessible polling places;
- equitable treatment of electors, candidates and parties by election officials, the government, the police, the military and the judiciary;
- an open and transparent ballot counting process, and
- an election process not disrupted by violence, intimidation or coercion.

Since no electoral event may be considered flawless in terms of the points enumerated above, the degree of impact of any positive and negative events must be assessed with the following questions in mind: *was the will of the majority of the voters expressed freely, clearly and knowledgeably and in secret, and did the election produce a government that is truly representative of the people's will?*

After taking all their observations into account, election monitors might ask themselves *to what degree* the election was free and fair, and *to what extent* it made a significant and positive contribution to the democratic evolution or development of the country concerned.

Elections: Not an End Unto Themselves

Unhappily, too many examples exist of electoral events which have not, in themselves, brought democracy to a country. This is because the infrastructures – social, economic, administrative, parliamentary and legal – were not sufficiently developed ahead of the elections, and/or because the right democratic 'mindset' had not yet evolved in the majority of citizens. Surely a prime example must be the sad experience in Haiti.

As Sir Anthony Siaguru, Deputy Secretary-General of the Commonwealth Secretariat pointed out at Wiston House: 'It would be unfortunate to confuse the end with the means and to forget that democracy implies far more than the mere act of periodically casting a vote. In essence, it covers the entire process of participation by citizens in the political life of the country.' At the same Conference, the Honourable Clive Griffiths, MLC, President of the Legislative Council of Western Australia and himself an experienced international election monitor, told participants: 'Elections are the lifeblood of any democracy. [But] the most technically successful "free and fair" election will be totally wasted if it does not lead to the successful establishment of a properly functioning democratic parliament and government.'

Parliamentary institutions are not inherently democratic; they need the external discipline of free and fair elections, as well as other checks, balances and appropriate internal procedures to prevent a relapse into oligarchy. Elections must result in the kind of transparency and accountability which are the indispensable characteristics of good governance. Thus it may be concluded that free and fair elections must lead to a representative parliament, but that a representative parliament depends on the holding of free and fair elections: the two are mutually inclusive.

Inevitably, free and fair elections are only a partial – though a very significant – expression of the fundamental political values which every society must embrace before it can be considered *truly democratic*. The wider need is to strengthen the structures of civil society which give sustenance to and are the lifeblood of a democratic culture.

In practical terms, as has been seen in Eastern Europe and other countries which have recently experienced their first democratic elections, disillusionment with democracy can set in if people do not have access to jobs and the basic necessities of life. It is no coincidence that, on the eve of victory in the historic South African election, president-elect Nelson Mandela was talking about just those practical issues as being the top priorities of an ANC government.

Beyond Free and Fair Elections

The fundamental challenge now, not only to the Commonwealth but to all the organizations which are actively involved in strengthening democracy throughout the world, is how to further a sustainable democratic process. As we approach the beginning of a new millenium, what are the prospects for continued international assistance to the democratization movement?

First, a people-centred vision of democratic development can be encouraged by closer international cooperation. The Wiston House Conference in 1994 followed from the earlier UN and Canadian-sponsored *Conference on the Coordination of International Assistance in the Electoral Field*, held in October 1992 in Ottawa and attended by delegates from 18 countries and 16 organizations and associations – parliamentary, governmental, non-governmental and commercial. Participants in this Conference recognized the desirability of coordinating the multitude of financial, material and technical assistance packages on offer to developing democracies; they strongly endorsed further exchanges of information, reports and experiences, particularly in the field of election monitoring.

The *Conference on Strengthening Democracy Throughout the World*, held 31 January–4 February 1994 at Wiston House, co-sponsored by the Commonwealth Parliamentary Association and Wilton Park Conferences, provided a further important forum for international consensus-building and policy development, not only for participants from the 22 member-countries of the Commonwealth, but for delegates from seven European countries, as well as the Council of Europe and the US.

There is no doubt that much has been learned in the 15 months separating the two aforementioned conferences. The international community is on a learning curve which has revealed the fact that, no matter how poor and poorly-educated people are, *they want to participate in elections; they want to practise the politics of inclusion.* But politicians in developing democracies must learn not to raise unduly the expectations of people about the immediate effects of instituting democratic processes in their countries. Free and fair elections on their own cannot ensure good governance, although they are a critical element in the process leading to it. Democracy means more than elections; emerging democracies and the international community alike might be well advised to look to developments in Namibia as an example of how a new democratic society may be created.

On a more practical note, hard economic times around the world and the limited human resources which can be made available in these cases lead to the conclusion that greater coordination of the work of election monitoring teams in future could prevent an unnecessary duplication of effort and waste of financial and human resources. Furthermore, more precise guidelines should be developed for use in assessing whether monitoring is advisable in particular cases and in evaluating the democratic process underway in respective developing countries.

4 Elections and the Representation of Minority, Aboriginal, Regional and Other Interest Groups (based on papers presented by the Hon Dr Paul Ssemogerere, the Hon Dr Howard A. Fergus and the Hon Ram Niwas Mirdha)

'... the zero-sum scenario that is associated with the winner-take-all (plurality) electoral system does, in my view, tend to over-reward the victor; and when the society has significant losing minorities and these are, by definition, ethnic minorities, ethnic tension is bound to be provoked.'
The Hon Dr Paul Ssemogerere, Second Deputy Prime Minister and Minister of Foreign Affairs, Kampala, Uganda, in his address to the *Conference on Strengthening Democracy*, 31 January 1994, Wiston House, UK.

'The Trinidad anthem proudly proclaims: "Where every pride and race have an equal place" *– a rhetoric which ethnic tension at election time and beyond belies.' 'We may ... need to revise our entire concept of democratic government to one that puts a premium on effectiveness rather than on time-honoured forms and formalities which leave many out in the cold. ... The challenge is to find a constitutional mechanism which sufficiently empowers the aboriginal people and other marginals and minorities, and ensures them an important niche in decision-making, while preserving the richness of the pluralistic culture which their presence imparts to the society.'*
The Hon Dr Howard A. Fergus, Speaker of the Legislative Council, Montserrat, in his address to the *Conference on Strengthening Democracy*, 1 February 1994, Wiston House, UK.

'It is quite clear that the choice of electoral systems has had a major impact on the emerging party system and the future of democratic government. ... The majority system produced a clear winner with an overwhelming majority of seats. Although it forced parties to build ethnic coalitions at the circumscription (constituency) level, the strength of the governing party leaves the future of the opposition in doubt. ... In the choice of electoral systems, short-term stability may have been exchanged for longer-term democratic development.'
Richard Vengroff in 'The Impact of the Electoral System on the Transition to Democracy in Africa: The Case of Mali', *Electoral Studies*, vol. 13, no. 1 (March 1994).

Context

There are many who consider that elections, while representing one step on the path to democratic development, can nevertheless exacerbate existing bitterness, divisiveness, alienation and powerlessness. These feelings can be brought on by the denial of human rights and political freedoms to minorities and regionalized groups within a society, as well as by their underrepresentation in parliamentary and other institutions and by their exclusion from the decision-making process. In some countries, opinion at election time is polarized on a racial, ethnic or regional basis and may result in open and violent conflict. In others, electors suffering such deprivations may simply abstain from exercising their hard-won democratic rights, either in protest or out of hopelessness and apathy.

The Commonwealth provides us with a wide variety of examples, ranging from countries like Nigeria and Uganda, whose populations are comprised of many or several different tribes each speaking their own language and sometimes practising different religions, to other countries whose populations have two or three distinct ethnic origins, such as Guyana and Mauritius, to yet others where geographic and/or historic factors have led to regional isolation and/or concentrations, like Trinidad and Tobago, and Antigua and Barbuda. Underrepresented and often socially and economically deprived aboriginal populations, making up only a minority of the total, may also be found in such Commonwealth countries as Australia, Belize, Canada, Dominica, Grenada and Guyana. A highly mobile population searching for improved personal economic circumstances, as is found in the Caribbean region, may complicate the situation even further.

Thus elections will often reveal unresolved fears and tensions in segments of a socicty which have previously been denied basic rights and freedoms and which see themselves as victims of systematic discrimination and/or oppression and lacking any political or legal recourse. Elections held in such circumstances may be perceived as 'competitions', raising the spectre of even more discrimination between 'winners' and 'losers'. The greater the rewards for winners and the greater loss for losers, the more likely it becomes that passions will be aroused, leading to conflict and further deprivations. For these very reasons, there are apparently well-intentioned advocates actually opposing democratization as a priority issue in Africa.[1]

The Role of the Electoral System in Exacerbating Ethnic and Regional Tensions

It can be seen that, where tension exists between distinct communities and where elections are held before the underlying causes of that tension have been resolved, the situation is likely to be aggravated if the electoral system employed is one which emphasizes adversarial relationships and minimizes prospects for broad-based consultation and cooperation.[2]

The system employed by most member-countries of the Commonwealth is, quite understandably, based on that used in Britain, namely, the plurality or first-past-the-post (FPTP) system. This embraces the winner-takes-all approach and the uninominal principle (i.e. single-member constituencies). A uninominal FPTP system has the potential for producing a clear electoral winner with a large majority and therefore a 'stronger' government, which in turn is more likely to lead to internal stability. However, in Africa, even when a party secures a clear majority of the votes cast, it may not be perceived as truly legitimate – for example, if significant minorities are left out of government, particularly if those minorities are ethnic or religious in composition.

As we shall see, proportional systems coupled with multi-member constituencies or a party list system with voting 'at large' reflect a high value placed on representativeness.[3] Such systems are therefore appropriate in circumstances where a parliament truly reflecting the ethnic composition of the population is of greater concern than the stability which might result from a large majority.

Electoral Systems: The Case of Mali[4]

A case in point is provided by the West African Republic of Mali, where the choice of electoral systems has had a major impact on the emerging party system and the future of democratic government. In fact, extraordinary changes in the past two years in Mali have led to the almost complete transformation of the political system. According to one observer,[5] most parties originally declared themselves in favour of a proportional electoral system. However, in the course of the discussions that took place in August 1991 during the National Constitutional Conference which inaugurated the democratization process, the spectre of an ungovernable system paralysed by an unstable legislative majority led the participants to accept a majority system. *Stability for the new democracy thus took precedence over the philosophical preference for proportionality.* As a compromise, proportionality was retained for the municipal elections.

The implementation of the two electoral systems is briefly outlined in the Appendix to this paper. Also included are the results of a *simulated* election illustrating the effect on the distribution of seats in the National Assembly if the 1992 votecount had been made in accordance with a proportional system instead of the majority system actually used.

The results of the proportionally-based municipal elections and the majority-based National Assembly elections in 1992 were very different. The results of the simulated proportional National Assembly elections would have necessitated a coalition government, the stability of which would be uncertain. The majority system, however, produced a clear winner with an overwhelming majority of seats. Although the system forced parties to build ethnic coalitions at the constituency level, the strength of the governing party now puts the future of the opposition in doubt. The possibility of the emergence of a government dominated by one party and the eventual drift to a one-party state are obvious concerns to both observers of and participants in the system. In the choice of electoral systems in Mali, short-term stability may have been gained at the expense of longer-term democratic development.

Exacerbating Ethnic and Regional Tensions Through Elections: Possible Remedies

Delegates to the *Conference on Strengthening Democracy* suggested a number of strategies for reducing the possibility of intensified ethnic and regional tensions at election time. These may be grouped into the three following general approaches:

1 Guaranteeing a proportionate representation of aboriginal, ethnic and regional minorities in the legislature;
2 Choosing electoral systems which are more likely to lead to increased representation of minorities and other special interest groups in the legislature; and
3 Reducing tensions and potential for conflict *before* elections are called.

1. Guaranteeing a Proportionate Representation of Groups

Proportionate representation of groups in a legislature may be achieved in one of several ways, assuming, of course, that those groups are ready and willing to participate in the political life of the country. Such representation may come about as a result of:

(a) establishing a minimum number of uninominal seats for a particular *region* where a minority is concentrated;
(b) establishing *special constituencies* in which only representatives of specific groups may vote and run as candidates;
(c) establishing *multi-member constituencies* where one or several seats in each constituency *must* be filled by a member of a particular group in society; and
(d) *nominating representatives* of particular groups to seats in the legislature.

An example of (a) is provided by Canada, where the constitutional formula for calculating the representation of the various provinces and territories in the House of Commons, rooted as it is in the principle of representation-by-population, is based on a starting point of a guaranteed fixed number of seats (75 out of 295) for Québec, the province where 75 per cent of Canada's francophone population[6] resides.

One way of guaranteeing the representation of aboriginal people or other minority or special interest groups in a legislature is to establish or set aside specific seats for representatives of the groups in question. These might be national or 'non-geographic', or they might be attached to or 'overlay' those regions which contain significant minority populations. Some would argue that aboriginal constituencies, for example, would marginalize and ghettoize aboriginal people or would isolate their representatives in the legislature, whereas others advocating such an approach hold up New Zealand's system of representation for the Maori as a positive example.

In Canada, where aboriginal people – Indian, Inuit and Métis – make up 3.5 per cent of the population, only 12 aboriginal persons (self-identified) have ever been elected to the House of Commons since Confederation in 1867. In its *Final Report,* issued in February 1992, the Royal Commission on Electoral Reform and Party Financing recommended the establishment of aboriginal constituencies as the best means of rectifying under-representation in the House of Commons while accommodating the wish of many aboriginal people for a greater role in Canada's institutions of governance.[7] The Commission said: '... *if Aboriginal people want to elect their MPs directly by voting in separate Aboriginal constituencies, the electoral system should accommodate this goal and should establish a framework to provide for its realization. ... Canada's past is replete with symbols of the exclusion of Aboriginal peoples from the Canadian polity. Eliminating discrimination based on law is not sufficient; symbols of inclusion are also needed.*' Constituencies established specifically for aboriginal people could provide such a symbol.

The Commonwealth provides further examples of legislated guarantees for minority groups: in Singapore, at least one candidate elected from multi-member constituencies must be a representative of the ethnic minority; and in Cyprus, despite the 1974 Turkish invasion and partition of the island, the Constitution still guarantees that at least 30 per cent of the seats in Parliament should be filled by representatives of the Turkish minority (whose seats now remain unfilled), while other minorities elect one member each.

Some observers make the point that multi-member (plurinominal) constituencies tend to produce a more balanced representation of groups in legislatures and favour the representation of ethnic minorities and women.[8] For example, it has been seen that culturally similar countries with multi-member constituencies of a substantial size have five times as many women in parliament as those with single-member electoral districts. There is also evidence to support the ethnic effect, with examples ranging from the German-Polish balance effected by the Hapsburg empire in Galicia in the early 20th century (using double-member constituencies) to the present situation in Britain, where many more local government councillors of ethnic origins are elected in the mostly multi-member wards of the London boroughs than in the rest of the country which generally does not use multi-member wards.[9]

It should be pointed out, however, that at the 1988 federal general election in Canada, where *single-member* constituencies are used for elections to the House of Commons, 48 elected members out of 295, or 16.3 per cent, belonged to the various ethnic groups which accounted for 23.6 per cent of the general population. Ethnic groups thus achieved an encouraging 70 per cent *of the objective of proportionate representation*, but visible minorities only 32 per cent and women only 25 per cent of that objective.[10]

A more certain method of guaranteeing the representation of minorities and other groups in a legislature is to nominate, or appoint, members from those groups. Nominated membership in parliament is commendable in some ways. In the opinion of one observer,[11] it can bring to government capacities, experience, intellectual resources and independent thinking which may not otherwise be available through the hustings and the party system; it can also give a genuine voice to the voiceless.

But for the nominative system to work well, care has to be taken in the choice of persons nominated and in who does the nominating. Following the fall of representative government in the Caribbean in the second half of the 19th century, nominated council members from the merchant-planter class merely buttressed gubernatorial autocracy and entrenched an oligarchy whose interests were opposed to those of the general population. On the other hand, if members are nominated by various *parliamentary* factions, care has to be exercised not simply to replicate the divisions of the elected group. We may be able to learn from the example of the Bermudan Senate in which five members are appointed by the government and three by the opposition; a further three, who hold the balance of power, are independently nominated by the Governor.

A further option involving nominated representatives, referred to earlier, is that of non-geographic national constituencies established to guarantee representation of special interest groups such as aboriginal peoples, women, trade unions and national religious organizations. However, since such groups are hardly ever discrete or mutually exclusive, consideration might be given to combining election and nomination. In other words, persons nominated by special interest groups could emerge from an elective process rather than be the choice solely of the person who nominates. Ultimately, if the method chosen is to nominate members, then some jurisdictions may have to go even further and seek to ensure that one or more of the nominated members are empowered to represent their constituents at the highest level of decision-making – in the cabinet or executive council.

2. *Choosing Electoral Systems to Encourage Representation of Groups*

As has been noted previously, multi-member constituencies and proportional representation do have the potential to elect ethnic and other minority groups more easily than majority systems. As an example, a comparison of 17 countries[12] illustrates that those with very low female representation elect their parliaments from single-member constituencies, whereas those with higher representation have proportional systems involving multi-member constituencies. Experience in Australia's federal and state elections with PR illustrates the point nicely. The rationale offered for the greater success of female candidates under PR is the significant reduction in obstacles that must be surmounted in order to become a candidate. Under the FPTP system in single-member constituencies, a party can select only one candidate, while in a multi-member constituency or in a 'voting-at-large' system using party lists of candidates, it is in the party's interests to select candidates who will have the widest possible appeal to all groups of voters.

The single transferable vote system[13] (with multi-member constituencies) may well produce the most representative parliament, though its complexity may be a drawback in countries where a significant rate of illiteracy exists amongst electors. When STV was first introduced in Malta, for example, about half the electors in some constituencies were illiterate.[14] In these cases, the voters were permitted to indicate their choices to the presiding officer in secret. However, the use of party symbols and logos, a practice which is already common in many new democracies, is an obvious solution to ensure that every voter may mark his own ballot in secret. In fact, in the historic 1994 South African elections, where electors voted for one party's list of candidates in a proportional system (national and provincial levels), a photograph of each of the party leaders was printed on the ballot, next to the name of the party and the party symbol. (The voter had only to make one mark on the ballot.)

Newly-emerging democracies seeking an electoral system that will lead to an equitable representation of all groups of society in parliament have many examples from which to learn. One of the most widely admired is the so-called *mixed* system in Germany which is a combination of separate uninominal and plurinominal elements but which is, at the same time, fully proportional. There are so many variations on the principle themes that, given a good grounding in all the pros and cons of the various electoral systems, it should be possible to find the right mix of elements to suit the society in question.

3. *Reducing Social Tensions*

In addition to adopting a suitable type of proportional representation for an electoral system, parties in contention at an election might be encouraged to reach certain agreements amongst themselves *before* an election is held.

In some newly-emerging democracies, powerful incumbents may fear for their future or even their lives in the event of losing office in an election. In addition, an important segment of society or the government – for example, the military – may be uneasy about the prospects of political change through elections. Under such circumstances the electoral programme might be sabotaged or rigged, which in itself may trigger ethnic conflicts.

One way of avoiding such an eventuality might be the negotiation, in advance of an election, of a power-sharing pact to guarantee some continuity for the incumbent. Another solution, which appears to have worked in Benin,[15] is an undertaking, backed by a law, granting immunity to the outgoing incumbent and his retainers.

The potential for ethnic conflicts associated with the electoral process might also be mitigated by elections which are seen to be free and fair, both at home and by the international community. Of great importance in this respect is the need to ensure that the 'playing field' is well and truly levelled for all parties before the commencement of the electoral process and that *all* the political parties in contention are fully consulted and involved in this endeavour.

Arguably the most important element of all in ensuring free and fair elections, however, is fully autonomous and independent electoral machinery, backed up by adequate human and financial resources and above reproach in terms of integrity and competence.

Concluding Remarks

It is important to realize that an electoral system, in and of itself, cannot be the sole means of preventing ethnic and regional conflict although, properly chosen, it can probably go a long way towards empowering, not only minorities, but the general population as a whole. In addition, once elected, the presence of representatives of minorities and other special interest groups in parliament does not in itself imply involvement in the decision-making process of government.

Rather, a holistic approach must be taken towards improving the economic and social conditions of deprived segments of society, with consideration being given to developing everyone to such a level that he or she may participate fully in society without having to rely on being singled out as a member of a particular population group. Furthermore, while new mechanisms, like electoral systems, need to be created, part of the solution must also lie in reorienting the mindset of some of our politicians. There is a morality involved in consulting the interests of minorities and aboriginal people which cannot be encompassed by legislation.[16]

In the words of the Hon Dr Howard A. Fergus, Speaker of the Legislative Council of Montserrat: 'In making proposals to remedy alienation and deprivation in parliamentary governance, we have to be careful not to confuse symbols and gestures with reality.'

Notes

1 The Hon Dr Paul Ssemogerere in his address to the *Conference on Strengthening Democracy*, 31 January 1994, at Wiston House, UK.
2 Ssemogerere, as above.
3 Michael Steed (1985), 'The Constituency' in J. Paul Johnson and Harvey E. Pasis (eds) (1990), *Representation and Electoral Systems*, Scarborough, Ontario: Prentice-Hall, Canada.
4 The following text relating to the case of the Republic of Mali is taken almost in its entirety from: Richard Vengroff (1994), 'The Impact of the Electoral System on the Transition to Democracy in Africa: The Case of Mali', *Electoral Studies*, vol. 13, no. 1, March, pp. 29–37.
5 Vengroff, 'The Case of Mali'.
6 1991 Census; single responses based on ethnic origin as opposed to usage of mother tongue.
7 Canada (1992), Royal Commission on Electoral Reform and Party Financing: *Communiqué No. 17.*
8 Enid Lakeman (1982), *Power to Elect: The Case for Proportional Representation*, London: Heinemann; also Steed, 'The Constituency' and Vengroff, 'The Case of Mali'.
9 Steed, 'The Constituency'.
10 Canada (1991), Royal Commission on Electoral Reform and Party Financing, *Research Studies*, Toronto: Dundurn Press. Alain Pelletier, 'Politics and Ethnicity: Representation of Ethnic and Visible Minority Groups in the House of Commons', Chapter 2 of Vol. 7, edited by Kathy Megyery.
11 The Hon Dr Howard A. Fergus in his address to the *Conference on Strengthening Democracy*, 1 February 1994, at Wiston House, UK.
12 Lakeman, *Power to Elect*.
13 A brief description is provided by J.A. Corry (1951), *Democratic Government and Politics* (2nd ed.), Toronto: University of Toronto Press: 'The single transferable vote requires a constituency with at least five members if it is to achieve its purpose of enabling each substantial minority to elect a member. Voters mark their choices in

order of preference, 1,2,3,4, and so on. The quota of votes necessary for election is determined* and, as soon as that number of first preferences is counted for particular candidates, they are declared elected and the remaining ballots for those candidates as first choice are transferred to the second choice and so on. When all surplus ballots have thus been transferred, the candidate with the smallest total is eliminated, and all his ballots transferred to the candidate who is the next choice on each. This process of transferring surpluses and eliminating the weaker candidates proceeds until the quota has been reached by as many candidates as there are seats to be filled.'

*The quota is determined by dividing the number of votes cast by the number of seats to be filled plus one, and then adding one to the result.

14 Lakeman, *Power to Elect.*

15 Ssemogerere, note 1.

16 Fergus, note 11.

Appendix: The 1992 Elections in the Republic of Mali*

A *proportional* electoral system was employed for the municipal council elections in Mali's 19 communes, elections which were held in advance of – and therefore were not influenced by – the National Assembly and presidential elections. However, a *majority* electoral system, based on a party list and a two-round election in largely multi-member constituencies (35 of the 55), was employed for the National Assembly elections.

Mali – Municipal Elections

None of the three strongest parties was able to capture a majority of seats or votes on any councils. With an average of eight different parties winning seats per commune, and with only one of the elections producing a majority party in a municipal council, *coalition-building* became an extremely important and complex activity. In the course of this process, a variety of trade-offs, several of which were to have an impact on the National Assembly and presidential elections, were agreed to. However, in the face of difficulties confronting the municipalities, the long-term stability of the municipal council coalitions remains to be seen.

Mali – National Assembly Elections

These elections were organized around a *majority electoral system* held in 55 circumscriptions (constituencies) in two rounds. The system requires each party to put forward a complete list of candidates equivalent to the

*Extracted from Richard Vengroff (1994), 'The Impact of the Electoral System on the Transition to Democracy in Africa: The Case of Mali', *Electoral Studies*, vol. 13, no. 1, March, pp. 29–37.

number of deputies (elected members) in each circumscription. Any party receiving a majority of the votes in the first round of the election in any circumscription is declared the winner. If no party receives a majority, the two parties finishing with the most votes compete in a second election one week later.

Results of the National Assembly Election Transposed into a Proportional System

If the votecount at Mali's 1992 National Assembly elections – run on a majority basis – is transposed into a proportional system, the result is a vivid illustration of what can happen to the distribution of seats among the parties.

Hypothetical Results of Mali National Assembly Elections Under a System of Proportional Representation by Region

Party	Seats won[1] (*actual*)	Seats won (*proportional*)	Net gain/loss
ADEMA	73[2]	43	–30
CNID	9	13	+4
USRDA	8	21	+13
PMD	6	2	–4
RDP	4	10	+6
UDD	4	4	0
Others	11	23	+12

1. Using a majority electoral system with party lists in multi-member constituencies in two rounds.
2. One seat won by ADEMA was declared vacant because of an ineligible candidate.

Change of Ranking of Parties

Ranking (first 6 parties only)	Party (seats won) *actual* results		Party (seats won) *transposed* results	
1	ADEMA	(73)[2]	ADEMA	(43)
2	CNID	(9)	USRDA	(21)
3	USRDA	(8)	CNID	(13)
4	PMD	(6)	RDP	(10)
5	RDP	(4)	UDD	(4)
6	UDD	(4)	PMD	(2)

As can be seen, if a proportional electoral system had been used in the 1992 elections in Mali, the National Assembly would have been left without a majority government: building a majority coalition would have required a minimum of 59 seats and the participation of at least three parties.

Although some would argue that a proportional system would be fairer than the current majority system, the latter clearly has some advantages, first and foremost being the greatly increased likelihood of electing a party with a clear majority of seats. Furthermore, the mostly multi-member constituencies under the existing majority system force the parties to incorporate diverse ethnic, familial and local interests. The parties in Mali that wish to assert influence *nationally* are therefore forced to build a relatively broad coalition of ethnic and regional groups. This system also acts as a safety valve, creating the possibility for regionally concentrated groups and their parties to win small blocks of seats.

5 Voter Education and Democratic Political Parties

'In order to change the attitudes of those who distrust authority and create a civil society, it is vital to educate the electorate as well as strengthen the democratic political parties.'
The late Johnson Ndlovu, MP, February 1994, Wiston House, UK.

Context

In papers presented at the Conference, the criteria for political democracy were held to include civilian rule effected through representative institutions and public liberties. Its components are, first, a legislative body periodically elected by universal suffrage, empowered to initiate it own legislation and to enact or repeal legislation initiated by the executive. The executive is thus subject to control and review. Candidates for the legislative body are normally members of contending political parties. Executive and legislative action is subject to periodic reappraisal through free elections, as well as being continually scrutinized by free mass media and other groups in society.

Within the legislative body, opposition and minority rights are guaranteed and governments can be changed in accordance with the constitution or some other set of prescribed laws. The emphasis of democracy lies on the society having the right and knowledge to vote, since democracy is government according to the wishes of the people, with public opinion expressed through recognized channels.

Political cultures vary considerably in the extent to which they encourage a sense of trust in political authority and facilitate political activity on the part of ordinary citizens. The ideal culture would be one in which the political ideas and attitudes of the citizenry were attuned to political equality and participation, and where government is seen as trustworthy and acting in the public interest. Such a political culture and such an attitude towards authority have the effect of disciplining a government in carrying out its responsibilities. They also influence patterns of cultural transmission such as education, economic relations, and family and kinship structures. When such a level of political and civil culture is attained, it can then be claimed that a civil society with a responsible electorate is in place.

Voting is the chief form of mass political expression in societies with competitive free elections. Whether individuals cast a vote out of traditional loyalties or for conscious pragmatic reasons, their choice can be a significant affirmation of identity with a particular group or sub-culture within the state. Votes also have direct consequences for government as they strengthen or weaken the position of leaders of organized political groups, especially minorities or special political interests, bargaining for power. Furthermore, the existence of free and informed voter participation within certain broad limits is considered as a logically necessary condition for the existence of democracy. In the absence of such behaviour, no political system could legitimately be called a democracy. Elections may also indirectly serve to reinforce official responsiveness to the public interest. Moreover, voting in genuine elections may be an important method of providing citizens with influence over policy and encourage their participation in its development. Participation is thus at the heart of the definition of democracy and of a civil society. The right to take part in government in a democracy means, at the very least, the right to vote by secret ballot in periodic elections.

A civil society offers its citizens basic democratic rights, the exercise of which largely guarantees human and political rights, including the representation of minorities. In the truest sense, the latter are thereby enabled to win over the electorate and come to power by peaceful means.

In the modern world, the concept of the democratic state has been superseded by that of the democratic society. Democracy is no longer simply a question of governing the state, but of running society in general. The features of this attitude are dialogue, confrontation of opinion, shared responsibility and participation in decision-making. It is no longer enough to elect and perhaps later replace the political leadership. All citizens should be able to have a voice in the management of society, starting with areas in which they are directly concerned. The role of citizens in the affairs of society does not expire after an election. In fact, democracy acquires a new dimension through people's participation in the day-to-day affairs of the country.

Voter Education and the Role of Political Parties

A basic presupposition for the development of democracy is the education and participation of its citizens. The spread of education allows the electorate to be made critically aware of relevant issues and problems, aware of the consequences and costs of past and present policies and alternatives for the future. Educating voters about their inalienable rights in a democracy is therefore an essential component of building a civil society.

Voter education can take several forms. As civic education, it provides information to the public on the basic system of government found in the country as well as the role and responsibilities of various institutions, be they judicial, legislative or executive. Specific voter education will instruct citizens on the exact procedure to follow as they conduct themselves through the voting process at the polls. It may also provide information on the intricacies of the electoral system. In some cases these programmes may be directed to the needs of specific groups of electors, for example first-time electors, though voter education programmes in many countries may be guided by the degree of illiteracy which prevails.

Political parties may also provide voter education. They may instruct voters on their own platform and policies or provide nonpartisan civic and voter education. When these voter education programmes are effective, they undoubtedly reinforce the interest of citizens in the process and possibly encourage a higher voter turnout at the polls.

In some countries, it was felt that these voter education programmes were not effective in inspiring sufficient numbers of electors to participate in the process. They therefore instigated a system of compulsory voting. Clearly, safeguarding a high participation rate gives to the electoral result a special political weight, a broad impact and a wider acceptance by society as a whole. The question arises, however, as to whether or not compulsory voting is fair to the electorate. One should then perhaps examine why some people do not vote. Some electors refuse to vote on the grounds that their party did not have a candidate and they could not justify voting for the opposition. Secondly, they might just be generally apathetic, not interested in political issues. Compulsory voting, however, forces the individual to make a choice. The greatest harm is done by the apathetic staying at home and thus allowing a minority who do care about the system to take over government.

In contemporary societies very often, the understanding, cooperation and common efforts of both political and social forces are needed to deal effectively with major issues and overcome difficulties. Democracy being a form of government based on public opinion, it must be organized and given a coherent form and direction to be effective. The accepted vehicle in modern democracies for this cooperation is the political party. It is the parties which bring together, and thus make effective, what would otherwise be so many diverse, yet like-minded, individuals.

A particular political party may emerge in response to the particular needs of the society in which it develops: it may emerge as a liberation movement or from followers of a charismatic leader. The task is to transform these movements or bodies into modern democratic political organizations.

Political parties assist people in the selection of representatives and leaders. In the absence of political parties, very few individuals would be able to mount an election campaign capable of reaching large numbers of voters across a modern state. Also, it is parties, rather than individual candidates, whose election manifestos, programmes and policies attract the support of voters. It is therefore necessary to strengthen political parties in order for more people to participate in decision making.

Democratic political parties can be strengthened by continuous dialogue within and without. Such dialogue will assist in introducing new ideas and clarifying issues inside and outside the party. The more people know about a party and its intentions, the better it is for that party and the public in general.

Candidate Selection

It was acknowledged at the Conference that although the selection and financing of candidates represent some of the most basic and significant activities in sustaining democracy, they were characterized by considerable differences in conventions, practices and legal processes and requirements. It was observed that the selection of candidates is one area in which very little democracy has traditionally been practised. This is because of the overwhelming role played by special interest groups and narrow networks of influential persons. It was noted that the selection of candidates is now increasingly being undertaken within the framework of a decentralized system of decision making which typically obliges constituency branches to nominate candidates. However, it was observed that, in many countries, the leaders of political parties continue to exercise a disproportionate influence on the selection process.

It was agreed that one of the major areas of concern involves the difficulty still being experienced in selecting a sufficient number of women to stand as candidates in elections. Attention was called to the quota systems, subsidies and other incentives utilized by political parties in Britain, Canada and Europe to redress this imbalance.

It was also observed that ethnic, religious and regional considerations were increasingly being taken into account as factors governing the selection process, and that this trend was likely to enjoy widespread application.

Election Financing

The Conference also discussed the financing of political parties. There was agreement that the practice of democracy required that money should not be able to buy political power, but recognized that inequalities in the distribution of financial resources between political parties was a factor which undoubtedly influenced electoral results.

In order to enhance the integrity of the political system under their authority, some officials have developed financial systems to strengthen political parties in their jurisdictions. The pressures which have encouraged the enactment of political financing regulations and public funding vary from country to country; what results in terms of regulations may vary as well.

In most cases, the allocation of public funds was deemed necessary to facilitate equality of opportunity and access to the electorate. Political parties and their candidates would then be freed from the need to obtain funds from questionable sources. Funds are needed desperately to establish and maintain offices and organizations, to provide research facilities and, most importantly, to fight effective election campaigns.

Regulatory Framework

Campaign subsidy schemes have rarely been adopted, however, without some type of regulatory measures also being put into place. Investigation has shown that party and candidate subsidies are never unconditional and have usually (but not always) been linked to a number of legal stipulations. These may require the reporting of details of income and expenditures, the audit of party and candidate financial records by public officials, and the publication of their findings. Limits may be imposed on particular types of expenses, and limits or bans on certain sources of funds. In addition, certain campaign activities may be completely prohibited.

Disclosure

In order to ensure that the expectations of the financing regulations are met, many countries require public disclosure or reporting. This enables public officials to determine whether expenditure ceilings and contribution limits have been respected, thereby assisting them in the allocation of public subsidies.

Many financial reporting procedures are restricted to the actual campaign period. In some jurisdictions, however, reporting must be done on an annual basis or even more frequently.

Funding Sources

In order to encourage the integrity of the political system under their authority, some officials have prescribed that contributions may come from only certain sources and must fall within specified amounts. An additional source of funds – the public subsidy – may be provided to reduce the influence of particular contributors and to permit less wealthy but otherwise serious participants to enter the electoral campaign.

Direct subsidies include grants of money to the parliamentary caucuses of recognized parties, annual allocations for organizational expenses, and cash advances or reimbursements for a portion of the total campaign expenses of qualifying parties and candidates. In contrast to direct subventions made for general purposes, specific grants or services are designed to cover part of the cost of direct expenditures. These include broadcasting, mailing, posting bills, paper, press and information bureaus, nomination meetings, women and youth groups or party educational and research foundations.

Indirect subsidies usually take the form of tax credits or tax deductions for contributions to parties and candidates, the reasoning perhaps being that this provides an incentive to parties to seek a broader participation of the electorate in the monetary aspects of the electoral process.

Concluding Remarks

It was concluded that many complex and difficult issues remain to be resolved regarding the financing of elections and the general activities of political parties. This was clearly an area deserving of continued study and reform in the interests of strengthening democracy internationally.

6 Agreeing a Representative Electoral Roll

'A voter registration system that is universally acceptable, protective of the interests of both the individual and the public, and widely perceived as fair and reasonable is one of the essentials of a free and democratic society. It follows that, to be accepted as legitimate, the procedures adopted by a democratic state to produce its lists of voters must themselves be known to be open, fair and free from abuse.'
The Royal Commission on Electoral Reform and Party Financing, Canada.

Context

Many of the organizations represented at the Conference have been instrumental in recent years in the observation of elections, specifically of polling day procedures. The agenda of this Conference, however, gave emphasis to another crucial element of the electoral process – the creation of the electoral roll. The agenda provided ample opportunity for the discussion of this aspect which, when examined closely, assumed considerable complexity. Indeed, one of the delegates commented that the registration process was a fundamental aspect of the election and in some countries may deserve as much or more attention than the actual voting on election day itself.

The registration or creation of the electoral roll may precede the election period by many months or only a few weeks. Certainly, the methods used to register voters, and the atmosphere surrounding this process can help to establish a positive environment for the process which follows. The creation of the electoral roll may be pivotal to the success of the ensuing election as well as to the long-term goal of establishing a basic structure to ensure that all those who are eligible to vote are properly registered for that purpose.

Purposes of Electoral Rolls

The usual purpose of an electoral roll is to ensure that all qualified electors are identified and that those who are so identified vote only as permitted by law. This protects the interests of the individual and of the public, while also serving to eliminate the potential for fraud or abuse of the system. In some countries, however, the right to include one's name on the electoral roll has been curtailed so as to keep certain groups from voting; elsewhere, registration is compulsory. The electoral roll may also serve a secondary purpose – as an informal population census. There have also been elections held (as in the Republic of South Africa) in the absence of an electoral roll. This requires special safeguards or at least unique procedures built into the voting process to prevent abuse.

For poll officials, the electoral roll becomes a very important tool. If the list is legible and accurate, it will help ensure that the exercise of the franchise by eligible voters is not impeded. It also allows the practical politician to identify areas of his constituency in which there is a low turnout and take remedial action. A final use of the electoral roll arises after the election when it can indicate voter turnout.

Methods of Creating Electoral Rolls

Excellent resources published in recent years describe the different types of registration and enrolment processes in existence. Very useful are the publications of the Canadian Royal Commission on Electoral Reform and Party Financing, specifically in its volume entitled 'Democratic Rights and Electoral Reform'; also a volume published by the Commonwealth Secretariat authored by Carl Dundas, *Organising Free and Fair Elections at Cost-Effective Levels*.

There are many different ways in which an electoral roll can be created. In the US, for example, the laws for voter registration vary from state to state, but the burden is essentially on individual electors to ensure that their names appear. In Canada, by contrast, the state takes the initiative in producing lists of electors. In the majority of Canadian jurisdictions, this is accomplished by an enumeration process which takes place during the election period itself. In Britain, there is a stipulated time for registration or changes in registration, after which the lists are in force for all elections (i.e. local, European Parliament and parliamentary) for as long as one year after a given date. Australia maintains a continuous electoral roll and enrolment is compulsory: everyone is obliged by law to apply for enrolment within 21 days of becoming eligible. Some European models are based on a system of national identity in which people must inform the authorities of a change of residence within one month of a move. In such a system, the public must accept that the police or other state authorities have the right to know where everyone is living. In many countries, the culture rejects this sort of public control over identity, even though such a system may produce the most accurate list of all.

Creating a Fair and Credible Electoral Roll

The CPA Study Group which met in Halifax in 1985 recognized that at the heart of determining the registration method lies a philosophical question: should the onus for registration rest with the state or with the individual? It also recognized that, although the relationship between the type of registration system chosen and the participation rate of electors is frequently studied, no satisfactory conclusions have ever been reached on this question. Whatever system is used to create the electoral roll, certain conditions must be met during its compilation to ensure that it is fair and credible. Observers must be satisfied that, on balance, the recommended conditions have been adhered to.

One can make the point that the closer to the date of the actual election that the electoral roll is being prepared, the more likely that considerations of accuracy will have to be sacrificed in order not to disenfranchise people. In some countries, too, the preparation of the electoral roll close to the actual date of the election might provide increased opportunities for fraudulent entries on the list. Since a well-prepared, representative electoral roll can act as a great confidence builder for the remainder of the electoral process, adequate time should be allowed for its preparation. On occasion, the election itself can be delayed because of disputes over a hastily or corruptly prepared electoral roll. Ideally, the list should be published well in advance of polling day, allowing ample opportunity for its examination and amendment.

Voter registration or enrolment must be conducted in an atmosphere conducive to a free and open process. This assumes that people are able to circulate freely and unimpeded. It also assumes an inherent understanding that basic rights and freedoms will be respected.

The Legal Framework for Enrolment

The process for the enrolment of eligible electors should be enshrined (well in advance of the commencement of the electoral process) within the legal framework governing the conduct of the election. This may be in the country's constitution, within the electoral law, within a piece of legislation dealing with the enrolment process itself, or in some other relevant statute. The process may also be governed by regulations which supplement the legal framework. It is important that the arrangements by which the process is administered are known and are acceptable to the citizenry. Preferably, the people may have been given an opportunity to make suggestions before these arrangements are enshrined. Such an opportunity would do much to ensure that the population has confidence in the process.

The legal framework would provide some basic standards for the conduct of the registration exercise. These could include the timing of registration in relation to the election date, together with the dates, hours and locations for registration and the personnel responsible. Most importantly, the qualifications for eligibility should be made known as well as the reasons for any possible disqualification.

Administrative Conditions Surrounding Enrolment

Even though the legal framework for the process may be readily accepted by all, it is also essential to determine whether the process is free from what might be termed 'administrative disqualifications'. Some examples are fairly obvious. People may be required to travel unreasonable distances to register. The times of the day when registration centres are open may place unrealistic demands on people, especially if they coincide with normal working hours. It also may be a hardship to obtain certain documents required to prove eligibility (such as a baptismal certificate, a passport, a national identity card, etc.). If photos are required as additional proof of identity, this can add further complications.

The Franchise and its Application

The rules for the qualification of electors and the criteria for disqualification will vary depending on the country's history, traditions and culture. However, it is important to ensure that these regulations do not unfairly discriminate against one group of people or benefit one group at the expense of another. Individuals may be disqualified for a number of reasons including mental disability (the individual may have been judged incompetent to handle his or her own affairs); physical incapacity; inability to read and write; a record of unethical or corrupt conduct (in many cases associated with election fraud or malpractice) and criminal behaviour (the individual may be held in a penal or correctional facility). Uncommon today as a requirement for eligibility is the ownership of property or having a certain income level. Clearly it is best if the right to registration is based on universal suffrage – clearly defined.

Within the domestic context, it is also essential to ensure that the rules are applied evenly and fairly across all sectors of the population, a situation which can be complicated by geography, remoteness from the administrative centre, or by poor communication facilities within the country.

Consideration may also have to be given to address the needs of citizens living outside the country. These are persons absent from their normal place of residence due to membership in the armed forces or the foreign service, or for economic or other reasons.

The Administrators

Equally important for the credibility of the registration process are the qualities and aptitudes of those responsible for its operation. The overall responsibility for administration may reside with a group of people (such as a multi-party electoral commission) or with one individual (such as a chief electoral officer). The function of registration may then be delegated to a more junior body or to someone like a registration commissioner who delegates tasks to registration officials. Whoever is responsible for the enrolment procedures must be seen as competent and efficient, and also provided with sufficient financial and human resources to carry out their tasks effectively. All those involved in the process must be well trained. It is also crucial that they are perceived as being reliable, honest and impartial. One must also try to discover if the personnel conducting the registration have been, or are likely to be, associated with any particular political party or element of the government. For example, if teachers or public servants are the registration officials, it is important to know whether they support certain government policies or if the population has reason to fear or be suspicious of them.

Enrolment: Accessibility

Another important characteristic of the process needing examination is the location where registration is carried out. It may be that certain locations, especially government buildings, are not conducive to building confidence in the minds of the electorate. In some societies, government buildings may be primarily associated with tactics of intimidation and control. In addition, although churches may instill confidence in some elements of the population and may seem appropriate locations for registration, other citizens may shun them for religious reasons. Sites must also be chosen for their central location since remoteness from population concentrations may inhibit the success of the registration exercise.

Enrolment: Timing

The timing of the registration process also plays a key role. The timing of the registration period in relation to polling day has a bearing on the process (as discussed earlier), as do the hours that the registration centres are open or when enumeration is carried out. Much depends on the working habits of the population. The time of the year also has an influence as it may be necessary either to avoid a major religious period or, if that is when many people are at home, to choose it. The general movement of people, for example of a migratory or nomadic society, may have to be estimated. In addition, weather patterns may have to be considered, as a registration undertaken in rainy/monsoon season or even in winter may not be desirable, given that the process may require people to be somewhat mobile.

Compiling and Distributing Electoral Lists

The electoral system together with the legal framework will determine the type of registration process to be used. The list may be compiled by constituency or, in the case of proportional representation, by a general registration of the electorate who are not tied to a particular electoral district or polling division. The methods used should be cost-effective but designed to meet the required end, which is the enrolment of as many qualified electors as possible. The end result – the list – should be standardized into some acceptable format: alphabetical order by surname, electors listed by address or electors listed numerically, based on their voter registration or national identity card.

Once the list has been compiled, it should be printed and distributed among the candidates, the political parties and the public to ensure as wide a circulation as possible. This must be carried out in good time to guarantee that interested parties have ample opportunity to peruse the list and attest to its accuracy.

Revising Electoral Lists

Circulation of the list will facilitate a review of its contents. Ample time should then be allotted for revisions to the list – allowing for additions, corrections, deletions and, if possible, the transfer of electors who may have moved in the interim. Such a period would also allow for objections to be filed against those who may not be eligible but were entered on the preliminary list. Any names registered as potential voters must be able to pass the test of subsequent verification and confirmation.

Enrolment: Appeals Procedure

An appeals procedure should also be integrated into the process. This would serve those whose names were objected to and deleted; it would also protect qualified electors who found that their names had been arbitrarily left off the list. The deletion of names (because of death, for example) must be done in accordance with standard and acceptable procedures to prevent incorrect or inadvertent removal. Also of importance is the need to ensure that, where rules are broken, appropriate penalties are imposed swiftly and impartially.

Role of Political Parties in Enrolment

The political parties may play a role in this whole process. For instance, political agents can nominate registration officials or provide manpower to scrutinize the process. Such supervision can ensure that the enrolment proceedings are carried out in an impartial and equitable manner. Some electoral systems may even allow political parties to encourage their supporters to participate in the registration process.

Enrolment Safeguards

Safeguards must be built into the system to guard against fraud which may include the forging and/or sale of identity documents. If identity documents are stolen from qualified electors, there must be some way for them to be easily replaced. Scrutiny of the documents and of the electoral list by concerned parties may also eliminate instances of illegal or double registration.

In order to protect eligible electors from fraud, some electoral systems provide what is termed a 'tendered ballot', a procedure followed if an elector goes to the polling station and finds that his or her name has already been marked off the list as having voted. Upon satisfying the poll officials that they are indeed the elector on the list, for example by showing identification, the elector will be provided with a ballot and two envelopes. The completed ballot will be placed in an unmarked unidentified envelope which thereafter can be treated confidentially. This envelope is then placed in another, outer envelope, which shows information pertaining to the elector, in case the ballot is later challenged. In other systems, electors in this situation may be allowed to vote simply by virtue of making an affidavit as to their identity.

Documentation in Lieu of Electoral Lists

For some electoral events (an election, a plebiscite or a referendum), it may not be possible to compile a list or register of electors. This may be due to such factors as timing or even cost. Different demands are then placed on the polling officials, the candidates and the political parties, as well as on any potential electors. Rules governing the standards for identifying electors must be well-defined. Any documents necessary to prove eligibility must be readily available.

Extra steps may have to be built into the voting procedure itself – to verify each document before a person votes and then invalidate it afterwards so that the document cannot be used by anyone else. In fact, the documents may have to be unique, containing the photo or some description of the voter. The document may have to be punched or stamped, and the voter may have to have indelible ink, or some other identifier applied to his or her person. Electors will have to ensure that they are in possession of the required document; electoral officials, political parties and candidates will have to be vigilant to ensure that the integrity of the process is upheld.

Enrolment: Role of Voter Education

Voter education is an essential component of the process. If possible, adequate resources should be allocated for the purpose of explaining the voter registration procedure and its importance in the overall electoral process. Such transparency may remove any fear or suspicion among the electorate and provide encouragement for wide participation.

Concluding Remarks

The optimum voter registration process will combine all of the elements enumerated above. Impartial officials will implement the procedure at acceptable locations and at times which provide maximum access for the potential electorate. Legal recourse will be inherent in the process, and voter education and appropriate polling procedures will reinforce the rules and regulations governing enrolment. All of these elements should be conducted in an atmosphere conducive to the development of democratic values.

The reality, however, may be somewhat different. Although many of these characteristics may indeed be evident, others may be lacking. It is therefore the duty of the observer to evaluate how far the process has been endorsed by the electorate and politicians, as well as its contribution to the entire electoral experience. It may not be possible to have a completely transparent enrolment process and to totally eliminate all possibilities of fraudulent activity. It may nevertheless be possible to foster a political culture within which fraud is unacceptable. The importance of agreement on an acceptable electoral roll by everyone involved cannot be underestimated. This may impact on the acceptance of the election results and outcome, as well as on the legitimacy and moral authority of those elected.

7 The Media and Elections: Ensuring Equal Access and Responsible Reporting[1] (based on papers presented by Colin Shepherd, MP and Patrick Keatley)

'Electoral laws promote fairness in the exercise of freedom of expression only to the extent that there are reasonable opportunities for citizens, particularly candidates, as well as political parties to present their case to other voters. Freedom of expression in this respect is crucial to the realization of the fundamental objectives of our electoral democracy. ... Freedom of expression ... is both a democratic right in itself and a means to the realization of other democratic rights. Free and democratic elections are not possible without freedom of expression.'
Reforming Electoral Democracy, Volume 1 of the final report of the Royal Commission on Electoral Reform and Party Financing, Supply and Services Canada, Ottawa (1991).

'Direct access programming[2] can help to level the playing field in order to create a fair and meaningful electoral contest. Biased broadcast campaign coverage, however, can shift the balance of political forces even where direct access programming has been relatively fair.'
Patrick Merloe in *Election Campaign Broadcasting in Transitional Democracies: Problems, Principles and Guidelines*, Article 19, the International Centre Against Censorship, London, UK (pre-publication draft, August 1993).

Context

Article 19 of the *Universal Declaration of Human Rights* acknowledges not only the right to hold opinions without interference, but also the right 'to seek, receive and impart information and ideas through any media and regardless of frontiers'. Three sectors of the population have critical rights of free expression to consider in the electoral context:[3]

- the potential voters and the general population,
- the news media, and
- the political forces that seek to compete for elected positions or otherwise to affect the outcome of the vote.

As Patrick Merloe points out, the electorate depends upon its right to receive full and accurate information. The print and broadcast media depend on their right to question and criticize the government, the candidates and the otherwise contending forces – free of censorship, intimidation or political pressures. And the political parties and coalitions depend on the ability to present their messages through the media freely and without distortion or manipulation and with an allowance of time sufficient for their messages to be understood.

Thus the media have a crucial role to play in the exchange of electoral information. However, aside from the level of evolution of a democratic culture, many different conditions, either on a nationwide basis or in certain regions of a country, may influence the significance of the role played by the media in election campaigns. Examples of adverse conditions and of election campaigns where such conditions came into play include the following:[4]

- an insufficient election period (Malaysia, 1990 and Albania, 1991, where campaigns were too short for political parties to establish themselves properly);
- limited availability of newsprint, ink and printing equipment for newspaper production, and the high cost of newspapers (Bulgaria, 1990);
- few newspapers, inadequate national distribution systems and unwillingness of incumbent political forces to deliver opposition materials to households (Romania, 1990);
- biased and politically-controlled media outlets which do not transmit certain parties' messages (Bulgaria, 1990);
- voter illiteracy leading to the heightened importance of radio (Namibia, 1989 and Guatemala, 1985 and 1990), and
- limited access to radio and television sets (Kenya, 1992, where 25 million people had access to only 82,000 televisions and 2 million radios; Chile, 1988 and 1989, where 80 per cent of the population had access to television).

Furthermore, specific actions taken by an incumbent government against the media can drastically reduce the significance of its role in an election campaign, and therefore also the possibilities of freedom of expression. Examples of such actions include the following:[5]

- censorship by government-controlled media (refusal to air opposition party messages or a requirement to change those messages, deleting critical broadcasts emanating from external sources);
- censorship by government agencies (central election commissions or broadcast regulation bodies);
- government banning of access to media by opposition parties;
- government closure of media outlets during election campaigns;

- government confiscations of campaign publications and detention of journalists on sedition charges;
- government threats of censorship leading to self-censorship by the media;
- imposition of martial law and states of siege by the government in order to permit censorship of the media or ban communications by other political parties;
- government intimidation by violent attacks and death threats on journalists (domestic and foreign);
- intimidation of journalists by arresting and detaining them;
- prosecution and imprisonment of journalists;
- attacks by political party supporters and failure of the government to protect journalists;
- attacks on and murder of journalists by political extremists (including governments) and the failure of government to protect journalists and prosecute those responsible.

As Patrick Merloe states,[6] the promotion of internationally-recognized standards to protect freedom of speech and the security of the person is imperative if actions of the type enumerated above are to be countered and eliminated. Standards which address such serious human rights abuses must be part of an effort to secure the media's role in promoting transitions to democracy. A government's failure to protect the media or to hold accountable those responsible for such abuses undermines the potential for free and fair elections; on the other hand, as the conveyor of many of the campaign messages, the media has a heavy responsibility to ensure fair, honest and impartial reporting of a campaign.

The Role of the Media in the Political Campaign

Effective media are, of course, crucial to the exercise of the right of freedom of expression. They are a potent tool at any time and serve several purposes during election periods: as providers of news coverage of the campaign, its issues and the players involved; as critical analysts of the campaign issues and campaigners, in public affairs programming and editorial comment; as a means of disseminating publicity about political parties, candidates and their campaigns, either through news coverage, or free and paid messages and advertisements; and as a means for potential voters to obtain information about issues, candidates, parties and the electoral process, which will help them to decide whether to vote and for whom. The extent to which the media are used in political campaigns in a given country, however, relates directly to their availability and to the access which the mass of the electorate has to them.

While politicians in developed democracies make extensive use of the print and electronic media, backed up by the use of posters (billboards), mobile loudspeakers, house-to-house canvassing and pamphleteering, political parties and candidates in newly-emerging democracies may still make extensive use of *public meetings and political rallies* to disseminate their messages. However it has been suggested that, even in those countries where the public meeting is still an important social event (e.g., Nepal, 1991), this form of campaigning is a time-limited phenomenon.[7]

In South Africa, for example, much attention was given by the parties to the *radio* dimension in the lead-up to the April 1994 elections, because the transistor radio is generally considered to be universally available there. In Britain, *poster (or billboard)* advertising is now considered by some[8] to be the most important advertising medium in elections, although the need to book billboard sites in advance means that the allocation of sites to the various parties may be less than fair.

Research conducted for the Royal Commission on Electoral Reform and Party Financing in Canada,[9] on the other hand, clearly illustrates the dominance of *television* as a vehicle for campaign communication in Canada, while noting that national political campaigns revolve around leader tours and media advertising. The same source also remarks on the trend towards television dominance as the most important – and trusted (rightly or wrongly) – source of campaign information for voters in virtually every industrial democracy. In terms of the influence of the media on the political process, their importance would seem to be in setting the agenda for the campaign and in influencing the basis upon which individuals make their decisions.[10]

Indeed, the way in which political parties conduct their campaigns in any given country is now largely a reflection of technological developments in the media and of the latest marketing principles and research, with the campaign usually being built around how the leader can be packaged and presented – very like the marketing of a commercial product. Much emphasis is placed on the personalities of the leaders and the conflicts between them, rather than on their political concepts. Especially in first-past-the-post electoral systems, candidates must identify with the issues through the 'leader's package' and ensure that their approaches reflect the package. The process is being further refined by the media's constant search for the all-important 'sound bite' – the pithy 'quotable quote' (becoming shorter all the time) particularly sought after by broadcast journalists for news reports.

Thus the relationship between the politician seeking election and the political commentators seeking to inform, analyse and even entertain is one of both symbiosis and conflict.

Ensuring Equal Access to the Media

> Each of the candidates or parties representing major strands of opinion should have access to the major instruments of communication for the dissemination of the message. This means not only that they must have the necessary finance, but also that those who control scarce resources – particularly the broadcasting companies – are regulated to ensure that they do not use their strategic position to control scarce resources as a means of excluding political views of which they disapprove.[11]

Politicians and political parties naturally seek the greatest possible exposure through the media during an election campaign. However, in multi-party democracies, it is reasonable to assume that there is always going to be a disparity in the relative sizes and financial capacities of the various parties. The question of reducing the disparity and equalizing access to the media during elections then becomes paramount. Various questions must first be considered and resolved in this respect:

- whether to allow or to disallow political advertising of any type in any format;
- whether to limit the amount of time and/or space that political parties may purchase for political advertising;
- whether to permit political advertising (for and against) by third parties and whether to put limits on overall election-related spending by political and third parties (special interest groups, associations, unions, etc.);
- whether to regulate the provision of free time and/or space in the media to parties for political advertising;
- establishing criteria for allocating paid and free time and/or space to parties for political advertising; should *all* parties (large and small, new and established) receive *equal*[12] time and space, or should past electoral performance (number of seats won) and/or the historical record of the parties be a factor?;
- whether to regulate the time of day (e.g. during prime time) at which air time must be made available by the broadcast media for the transmission of paid and free-time political messages;
- whether to allow political advertising outside electoral campaign periods as well as during the campaign, and whether to prohibit or restrict it (advertising blackouts) to certain periods during the campaign.

The practices of democracies around the world in respect of regulating the use of media by political parties and candidates are as different as the countries themselves. In fact, many more countries legislate the provision of free broadcast time to political parties than permit parties to purchase air time. (Canada is an example of one country which provides for both.) The rules for the allocation of free time among parties differ quite widely. The most common pattern is for the time to be allocated among the parties represented in the national legislature on the basis of the number of seats held or the share of the popular vote received in the previous election or a combination of the two.[13] In Canada, for example, the criteria used in the allocation of free and paid time to Canadian political parties by that country's Broadcasting Arbitrator at the 1993 federal general election were based on 'statutory factors' (the percentage of seats held by parties in the House of Commons, the percentage of the popular vote garnered and the number of candidates endorsed by each of the registered parties in the previous general election) and on a recent court decision which ruled that the allocation formula had a discriminatory effect which favoured established parties at the expense of new or emerging parties.[14]

Outlines of the widely-differing provisions for political advertising in the broadcast media made at recent elections in various transitional democracies have been compiled by Patrick Merloe.[15]

Financing Political Party Access to the Media

As Patrick Merloe points out in the context of the broadcasting media,[16] political advertising costs money. Direct access for political parties (defined as 'free' time slots or paid advertisements) must be paid for either by the government, by the broadcast outlets themselves or by the political parties.

The problem then becomes the fair and proper allocation of campaign resources. This may be complicated by a lack of national resources, as well as by the issue of the government's proper use of its regulatory powers over privately-owned media. The governments of some transitional democracies have allowed the purchase of air time, but this should be considered only as *supplementary* to the provision of free time because of the possibility of opposition parties being prevented from purchasing time on broadcasting facilities which, in those countries, are often state-owned.

In consequence, Merloe concludes that it is proper for a transitional government not only to expend national resources to pay for air time on both government-owned and privately-owned media, but also to use its regulatory powers to require private media to provide air time to political parties on an equitable basis during an election campaign.[17]

A more pervasive problem in allowing the purchase of air time is that some parties, including the ruling party, may have distinct financial advantages over their opponents and thus the ability to purchase disproportionate amounts of time. Campaign finance controls (such as those practised in established democracies like Australia, Canada and Germany) can be used to lessen this discrepancy, but they often are not in place during a country's transitional process.

As Merloe points out,[18] no matter which methods of qualification and time allocation are formally adopted, problems may still emerge during implementation. Obviously, the formulae devised to qualify parties for access to time, to allocate blocks of time and to assign time slots must be fair and established well in advance of an electoral event. Furthermore, access to production facilities (preferably the same ones) must be made available to all parties who qualify for broadcast time.

Responsible Reporting of Election Campaigns

> While some transitional democracies may have the advantage of an experienced media steeped in the traditions of independent journalism, this is often not the case. Even where government interference or pressures on the media are slight, news media inexperienced in independent journalism are bound to have difficulty in fulfilling their roles in election campaign coverage. Even more striking are cases where the government and the media endeavour to present a biased picture to the people in order to perpetuate the control of the ruling powers.
>
> Election campaign coverage problems are varied. Some are subtle, while others are obtrusive. Most revolve around the central issue of whether the incumbent powers approach the electoral process in good faith.[19]

Merloe identifies three principal problems with media coverage of election campaigns in transitional democracies, namely:

- imbalanced coverage;
- failure to distinguish between government activities and campaigning; and
- manipulation of coverage.

Imbalanced Coverage

This is the most prevalent problem in transitional settings – both quantitatively and qualitatively. Most often, the governing party receives considerably more coverage than the opposition. At the same time, the governing party may be presented in a disproportionately favourable light, while the opposition is presented negatively. Such imbalances can be avoided if the major news media draw up formulae for equitable coverage of the major contenders (as was the case in the 1991 election in Bangladesh), and if the government instructs the media to be impartial in covering the parties and candidates.

Failure to Distinguish Between Government Activities and Campaigning

It is essential that the media distinguish between government officials carrying out newsworthy government functions and the same people conducting election campaign activities.

Officials will often deliberately schedule government activities in order to gain media coverage during an election period. They may also appear at campaign rallies and give political speeches at meetings of civic organizations during the campaign period. The line between government functions and political campaigning is therefore not always clear. Consequently, the media have to be vigilant; they should not automatically accept an official's categorization of an event as a government function. Similarly they should be on the watch for more subtle attempts to take advantage of situations in order to gain publicity. For example, in the 1990 election period in Guatemala, the symbol of the President's political party (rather than the national seal) was displayed on the television screen following the President's addresses.

Manipulation of Coverage

Sometimes it is apparent from the degree of imbalance in news coverage that the media have consciously attempted to influence the outcome of an election. In such cases, news and information programming seem to be aimed at manipulating the impressions of potential voters. Merloe cites examples in Albania (1991), Kenya (1992), Namibia (1989), Korea (1987) and Taiwan (1991). The problem raised is how and where to intervene in media practices.

The Case for a National Media Code

The issue of media accountability is a controversial one in the *developed democracies*, where any efforts to impose standards on news reporting are seen as attempts to stifle freedom of expression.

A good illustration of that controversy may be found in the final report of Canada's Royal Commission on Electoral Reform and Party Financing,[20] where it was reported that journalists debated heatedly during a media practitioners' workshop as to whether self-policing should be a collective undertaking and whether a common set of standards could ever be adopted unanimously. The commissioners noted that 'the only evidence of unanimity was in the universal antipathy to government regulation of journalists during elections'. However, the Royal Commission remarked favourably on a number of initiatives taken in Canada in the field of media accountability. These included the existence of many provincial and local press councils in Canada; the efforts of the Fédération professionnelle des journalistes du Québec towards the professional development of journalism and its adoption of a charter of journalism; the Canadian Broadcast Standards Council's 'Code of Ethics'; the Canadian Daily Newspaper Publishers Association 'Statement of Principles for Canadian Daily Newspapers'; the 'Code of Ethics' of the Radio-Television News Directors Association of Canada; the establishment of an 'ombudsman' at the Canadian Broadcasting Corporation and in five Canadian daily newspapers; and the efforts of several dailies to develop codes of conduct. In Britain, a recent move towards accountability of the press has led to the formation of the Press Complaints Council.

As has been pointed out by Patrick Keatley,[21] while the media quite naturally favour a minimum of restriction on their activities, in *developing* countries the need often exists for ground rules and the protecting arm of government in order to confront the hazards of bullying tactics. Preventitive measures can include the following:

- The formation of media associations well ahead of an election campaign, in order to facilitate discussions with the authorities and ensure the personal safety of journalists, both domestic and international.
- The institution of a formal system of media accreditation and issue of passes, undertaken either by the local police force or journalistic associations such as the Commonwealth Journalists Association (CJA), in order to avoid the problem of political party partisans masquerading as journalists.
- The development of a national code for the media, including measures to ensure compliance and enforcement.

The Role of External Media

Until such time as the media can properly establish a role for itself in any developing country, external media sources can play an important part in backing-up rather weak, newly-established local media. Stories filed by international journalists to their home countries and sent back to the country of origin through satellite transmission or the international press, can often result in positive action being taken to rectify unfair situations. In fact, international satellite television transmissions have had the effect of breaking down barriers and providing the fuel for local media to argue their own case in the face of repression.

Developing Journalists of Quality: The Role of Training

It is arguable that a vigorous media is an essential bulwark for democracy, which means standing up against censorship and asserting rights of access, both during and outside election campaigns. Jefferson said: 'The price of liberty is eternal vigilance.' Developing countries need the media to be the critical watchdog that they are in the established democracies and industrialized societies. Political leaders and other decision-makers in those countries respect the power wielded by the media, but they need to know that their respresentatives are as well-educated and informed as they are themselves before that respect may be earned.

There is little doubt that training is the key to a well-informed and professional media corps, but this is a long-term activity and requires commitment. Several organizations have grasped this lesson and have come to grips with the challenge. Included are the German foundations which finance fellowships that include media training, and the European Community equivalent working from Brussels. Arguably, the Commonwealth has led the way in this area for many years. Starting with the institution of its exchange plan soon after being founded in 1910, the Commonwealth Press Union (CPU) provides briefings and training sessions, while the Central Office of Information does the same at government level in the UK. Through the Commonwealth Media Development Fund, the Commonwealth Secretariat also provides funding for media training.

As of January 1994, the Commonwealth Journalists Association had laid the groundwork by providing 64 courses in every region of the world. To buttress its independence and augment the scope of its operations, the CJA has recently formed the CJA Trust, a registered UK charity which, starting with the 48 Commonwealth countries, is hoping to expand and offer its services globally.

Such efforts need to be promoted and expanded in order that the media in the new democracies may perform their crucial functions in a fashion that is satisfactory to all involved – the political parties, the electorate and the media outlets themselves. As Patrick Merloe has stated, the news media have a crucial role to play:

> Democracy depends on all contesting points of view being fairly and equitably communicated so that the people may make informed choices. The ability of the opposition, in addition to governing forces, to avail itself of the news media is critical in this regard. There cannot be meaningful and vigorous debate of fundamental issues facing a country without a vehicle for widely expressing views. The news media provide that vehicle in many instances.[22]

Notes

1 This text draws freely on the contents of *Election Campaign Broadcasting in Transitional Democracies: Problems, Principles and Guidelines*, prepared by Patrick Merloe for Article 19, the International Centre Against Censorship, August 1993 (pre-publication draft). As far as possible, this and other sources are acknowledged in the relevant sections of the text.

2 Includes both free time and paid advertising.

3 Patrick Merloe (1993), *Election Campaign Broadcasting in Transitional Democracies.*

4 *id.*

5 *id.*

6 *id.*

7 Colin Shepherd, Conservative MP for Hereford, in his address to the *Conference on Strengthening Democracy*, 3 February 1994, at Wiston House, UK.

8 Martin Linton (1994), *Money and Votes*, London: Institute for Public Policy Research.

9 Frederick J. Fletcher and Robert Everett (1991), 'Mass Media and Elections in Canada', chapter 7 of volume 19 (*Media, Elections and Democracy*) of the *Research Studies* of the Royal Commission on Electoral Reform and Party Financing, ed. Frederick J. Fletcher, Toronto: Dundurn Press.

10 R.H. MacDermid (1991), 'Media Usage and Political Behaviour', chapter 2 of volume 18 (*Media and Voters in Canadian Election Campaigns*) of the *Research Studies* of the Royal Commission on Electoral Reform and Party Financing, ed. Frederick J. Fletcher, Toronto: Dundurn Press.

11 Keith D. Ewing (1992), *Money, Politics and Law: A Study of Electoral Campaign Finance Reform in Canada*, Oxford: Clarendon Press.

12 The issue of *equal* time raises the issue of *equitable* treatment of political parties. As the Canadian Royal Commission on Electoral Reform and Party Financing pointed out in its final report: 'The regulatory authorities periodically remind broadcasters of their obligation to provide equitable treatment. Equitable, however, does not mean equal. It pertains to the fact that all candidates and parties are entitled to some coverage that will give them the opportunity to expose their ideas to the public.'

13 Fletcher and Everett, *Mass Media and Elections in Canada.*

14 Appendix C – Report of the Broadcasting Arbitrator in *Towards the 35th General Election: Report of the Chief Electoral Officer*, Ottawa: Elections Canada, 1994.

15 Patrick Merloe (1993), *Election Campaign Broadcasting in Transitional Democracies.*

16 *id.*

17 *id.*

18 *id.*

19 *id.*

20 Canada (1991), Royal Commission on Electoral Reform and Party Financing, *Reforming Electoral Democracy: Final Report (vol. 1)*, Ottawa.

21 In his address to the *Conference on Strengthening Democracy*, 2 February 1994, Wiston House, UK.

22 Patrick Merloe in *Monitoring Media Fairness in Election Campaigns: An Introduction to Basic Issues*, Washington, DC: National Democratic Institute for International Affairs (January 1994).

8 Election Observation (based on papers presented by Dr Horacio Boneo and Mr Patrick Merloe)

'Parliamentary institutions are not democratic per se. *Without the external discipline of free and fair elections and other popular checks and balances – as well as appropriate international procedures – Westminster-style Parliaments would veer towards oligarchy just as surely as did the Soviets of the former USSR.'*
The Honourable Clive Griffiths, MLC, in his address to the *Conference on Strengthening Democracy*, January 1994, Wiston House, UK.

'The presence of ... observers may contribute to the credibility or legitimacy of an election ... [and] can play an important role in helping a country achieve the objective of becoming a multi-party democracy.'
'Towards free and fair elections – the role of international observers', Ron Gould, *IN FOCUS,* Vol. 2, No. 9, February/March 1994.

Terminology

At the outset, it would be useful to clarify the terminology to be used for the purposes of this chapter. 'Observation' is a separate and distinct activity from technical assistance. 'Observation' should not be confused with the supervision and verification of elections. Furthermore, to avoid confusion, the term '*observation*' will be used as distinct from '*monitoring*'. 'Monitoring' is generally used in situations where a more active role than that of an observer is involved; monitors often have the authority to advise, consult and sometimes negotiate with the parties concerned. On the other hand, the observer's role is to act in a more passive capacity. In practice, the United Nations only uses the term 'observation' where full geographical coverage of an electoral event is required.

Why Observe? – Objectives

The clientele for international observation can be divided into two groups, namely, *external* and *internal*. External 'donor' clientele are those groups and organizations which have an interest in the democratic development of the country concerned, arising out of considerations such as human rights, the opening up of societies and long-term political and economic relationships. There can be various internal 'recipient' clienteles: the existing government of the country which wishes to obtain an international stamp of approval on its electoral initiatives for political, economic or other reasons; opposition parties looking to international observation as a means of discouraging intimidation and fraud; electoral authorities for support and defence against unjust accusations, and the public for security and confidence building. With some variations, these are generally accepted international reasons why states participate in election observation.

From the point of view of the 'donor', the observer's role is to form an opinion on the electoral process and to produce an internal report and often a public statement evaluating the freeness and fairness of the electoral process. This evaluation may influence subsequent relations between the donor organization or state and the 'recipient' state where the election took place.

From the perspective of the 'recipient', observation can serve to deter fraud and irregularities, thereby increasing the integrity of the process itself. Observers can facilitate communications and dispute resolution where individual parties complain to them by providing information to the officials responsible. Even though they may have no authority over the voting process, the very presence of national and international observers often adds a degree of moral suasion that acts as a dampening influence on violence, intimidation and other infractions. The involvement of both national and international observers can have a positive impact on increasing public confidence in the voting process, and may have a direct influence on increasing voter participation as well.

There are a number of approaches to raising public confidence in observers and correspondingly in the voting process. One effective technique concerns the involvement of high-profile and well-respected international observers such as ex-President Jimmy Carter. Publicly and frequently displaying the flag or logo of the multilateral organizations involved, such as the United Nations or the Commonwealth, can serve to demonstrate the interest and concern of the international community. This can be reinforced by emphasizing the credibility of the observer group, through informing the public on the roles and responsibilities of observers, and through publicising periodic reports by them, preferably throughout the election period. Finally, the provision of hundreds and even thousands of national and international observers present at the majority, if not all, of the polling stations serves to give a sense of comfort and confidence to the voters as they cast their ballots.

Observation can be used as a vehicle to guarantee the electoral process and give support to the regime of the state where the election is taking place, or it can do the opposite – denounce a situation and thus condemn a regime. It can also serve to help improve subsequent elections in that country and possibly even in others.

Who Observes?

Observers can be classified into two principal groups: national and international. Within these main classifications, there are a wide variety of observer groups.

At the *international level*, there is the possibility of observers from one country being part of the following: of a bilateral group officially representing the donor nation; of a multilateral group such as the United Nations, the Commonwealth, the Organization of American States, etc; of a non-governmental organization such as church groups or human rights organizations; as well as diverse VIPs and other individuals.

At the *national level*, the principal observer groups are usually formed from non-governmental citizen organizations such as church groups, lawyers groups or human rights organizations, specifically combined and trained to observe the election process. Political parties and their representatives at the polls play a critical role, as does the media where it is free and independent. In a few instances, the responsible electoral body is charged with organizing a national group to observe and sometimes to monitor the electoral event.

The presence of international observers is no substitute for the active involvement of party political representatives and national observers. For example, where national representatives can normally be present at every poll in the country for the duration of the voting period, there are usually too few international observers for them to be present at all polls; they generally do not remain at one specific poll throughout the process but visit numerous polls in a given area.

Unlike national observers who are usually knowledgeable about the political and electoral environment, well organized and coordinated, and who, in these situations, can evaluate the election on the basis of common criteria and standards, international observers are a diverse group from many countries and organizations, with a wide variety of experience (or lack of such), approaches and standards. Some will have no comprehensive knowledge of the country and its electoral environment, while others will have certain preconceptions and biases. There is seldom a common evaluation of an electoral event by international observer groups whose election observation activities are, in numerous instances, conducted independently with little or no intergroup consultation or coordination.

Rights and Responsibilities of Observers

In his paper entitled 'Rights and Responsibilities of Observers',[1] Pierre Cornillon states the following:

> ... An observer must only observe; he is a witness. While he may sometimes serve as a catalyst, he must never become actively involved in the electoral process.
>
> Observers bear a heavy responsibility, not only towards the international community which undertakes to make appreciable financial efforts and mobilizes important human resources, but also towards the people of a country who often place great hopes in them. Their action must therefore satisfy three key qualifications: *diligence*, *independence* and *impartiality*.

Mr Cornillon argues that, in order to carry out their mission 'diligently, independently and impartially', international observers must fully enjoy that fundamental human right known as *freedom of movement*. They must therefore be able to travel throughout the national territory and, if circumstances so require, accept the necessary guarantees for personal security.

This freedom of movement would of course be meaningless if it did not go hand-in-hand with the possibility of *receiving and communicating information*. This right to the *cooperation of the authorities* has many aspects. It implies that observers can talk freely with any citizens, as well with candidates and representatives of the political parties, with various associations and groups, with representatives of the public or private media and with representatives of the authorities and electoral officers.

In order for them to form an opinion, it is also essential for observers to have *access to all documents and material* relating to the electoral process. These include not only the legal texts and provisions governing the entire process, but also such essential elements as the electoral lists and rolls and voters' registration cards. Observers must of course be able to examine, if possible in advance, the whole range of electoral material, starting with the ballot boxes and ballot papers which are to be used, the kind of posters authorized, etc.

The right to have access to these documents and material must be backed up by a right of *access to premises*. This refers not only to the various meetings and rallies held during the campaign, but also to the polling stations and counting centres during the tallying of the vote. In some situations, the transport and safekeeping of ballot boxes in total security and confidence may be a very delicate issue. It is therefore extremely important not only for observers to have access to the places where the boxes are stored, but also for them to be able to accompany the boxes on their journey between that place and the polling station if the voting is spread over several days, and certainly during their transport to the centres where the ballots are to be counted.

The right of observers to receive the necessary information from the electoral authorities and from those in charge of security or the maintenance of order includes the right to receive information from them not only on complaints that may have been lodged, but also on the follow-up action taken on such complaints or other claims. The corollary of this right is twofold: the possibility and the duty to inform those authorities as swiftly as possible of any irregularity or incident which they may have witnessed or which was pointed out to them in good faith. Here, again, they have a right to receive answers to their questions. This must, of course, be done within the strict limits of their role since observers must refrain from any interference in the organization or carrying out of the elections.

The observers' fundamental responsibility of presenting their findings in a final public report implies both that they must submit the report to the authorities and that they are free to make its contents public in the country.

The exercise of rights and the liability to obligations imply that those concerned be clearly identified. This raises the question of the *accreditation* of observers. It seems highly necessary that foreign observers should undertake a formal accreditation procedure which confers a formal status on them. The first merit of official accreditation is to guarantee that, in coming to a country, an observer is responding to an invitation, whether issued personally or more generally. Such a procedure helps to define the rights and obligations of the accredited person (and may even specify and make public certain prohibitions on his action). It thus has the merit of giving rise to the adoption of legislation or regulations which establish an official relationship between the observer and the country's authorities.

The spectrum of institutions which send or may wish to send observers is very broad. It is therefore quite conceivable that, in the matter of accreditation, a State may distinguish between several categories of observers, each having more or less extensive rights and facilities. While the guarantees offered to all categories must never fall short of the minimum needed for observers to carry out their responsibilities, it is only natural that personal privileges will vary. It is therefore possible that, in some cases, observers may enjoy privileges identical to those afforded to diplomats under the Vienna Convention.

Accreditation must involve issuing observers with visible and distinctive means for their identification; these may be in various forms but must include an identity card. This enables them both to confirm their status in order to take advantage of the rights accorded to them, but also to be readily identifiable to the population while carrying out their activities and, if necessary, to benefit from certain personal security guarantees.

Since accreditation establishes the minimal obligations which observers must respect, a process for the withdrawal of accreditation is foreseen to punish serious and clear-cut cases when observers fail to respect their obligations or the general code of conduct. However, the threat of such withdrawal should not prejudice the actions of observers nor the exercise of their right of expression.

Although it is not a widespread practice, some States have a Code of Conduct which defines the rights and responsibilities of observers to which they must subscribe as a condition for accreditation. Most of these Codes of Conduct deal with the factors described above but may also include additional provisions pertaining to non-interference in the jurisdiction or affairs of the State and a promise not to disrupt the voting process at the polls. A summary list of 'Terms, Conditions and Code of Conduct for Observers' is described in the *Reference Guide for Election Observers* (Appendix 1).

Methodologies of Observation

> Only amateurs observe elections on election day. Professionals are involved well before.

Observation must cover the entire electoral process including registration of parties, candidates and voters, the political campaigning, the voter education and information process, media activities, the training of electoral officials as well as polling day activities, the counting of votes and the proclamation of results.

The different methodologies of observation can be described and evaluated in terms of three dimensions, the first being *chronological coverage*. This involves covering the whole process from legislative development through election day to the proclamation of results. This is done directly by only a small minority of observer groups. In lieu of direct involvement, an alternative approach is chronological reconstruction in the case of short missions. This is achieved by discussing the evolving process with political parties, technical assistants or other groups and organizations which have been in the country throughout the electoral period or by sending in advance teams or carrying out periodic visits to obtain briefing information. Direct involvement implies a permanent presence moving throughout the country such as has been done by the United Nations and Commonwealth.

The second dimension is that of *geographic coverage*. Often, because of their limited numbers, observer groups, can visit only a few of the major cities or areas of the country concerned. In order to obtain the required comprehensive information, coordination with other groups and use of a network of contacts across the country will often serve to fill much of the information void.

The third observation methodology involves the use of both *primary and secondary sources of information*. Primary sources include election officials, political party officials and other observers who can provide first-hand factual information on the process or activities which they attend. These are much more important and tend to be much more reliable than secondary sources which convey information on matters which they did not personally experience and thus may not be reliable.

What is Observed?

As democratic development often starts with law reform, observation should begin with a review of the electoral law and regulations. Subsequently, observers should evaluate the way in which these election rules are being administered by the responsible election body. It is important to understand how the country has been divided into districts by electoral boundaries, and the fairness of these boundaries, for the purposes of representation. Similarly, the fairness and comprehensiveness of the electoral lists should be carefully examined, and a determination made as to whether political parties and civic organizations have participated in the process of compiling them. The effectiveness of the voter education process is critical in informing the electorate on how to register, how to check their registration and where and how to vote.

During the period leading up to and including the election, it becomes essential to observe whether parties, candidates, electors and observers have freedom of movement and expression; the degree of freedom of média reporting; the integrity of the balloting and counting processes; the complaints process and, finally, the proclamation of results followed by the accrediting of parties and the installation of candidates.

All of the above must be carried out with objectivity and impartiality, using first-hand factual information as the basis of observation wherever possible.

Coordination of Effort

Over the past several years, there has been an increasing emphasis on consultation and coordination, especially involving multilateral groups, as well as some bilateral and NGO observers. This matter was the subject of a United Nations-sponsored conference held in Ottawa (Canada) in 1992.

Some examples of effective coordination include the role played in Kenya by the United Nations in acting as a central focal point for any and all organizations that wished to coordinate their observation itineraries and avoid duplication of effort. Briefing material was prepared and made available, and the United Nations team acted as a resource and administrative service for all interested observers. In Pakistan, the National Democratic Institute (NDI) made available reports, hotel addresses and telephone numbers; it also indicated where observers might be assigned to effect maximum coverage. This coordination service was provided to the Commonwealth, the European Union and national Human Rights groups. In Niger, the United Nations and NDI jointly coordinated all delegations. In some cases, the coordinating bodies also facilitated meetings of the various observer groups, both prior to and following the election. In the former case, the meetings were for the purposes of briefing the observers, and providing information on the most recent developments and problems arising prior to polling day. In the latter situation, the meetings were designed to facilitate the exchange of experiences and views. However, the actual reporting mechanisms and the reports themselves were carried out and prepared independently by each of the observer groups concerned.

With the ever-increasing number of observer organizations becoming involved in elections, the majority of which arrive only just before polling day and leave shortly afterward, the need for coordination is becoming increasingly critical. For example, it provides a vehicle for consulting and comparing findings after the election, and for minimizing the risk of coming to conclusions and making public statements based on limited observation, on third-hand information and, worst, on rumour.

Reports

Many articles have been written, and many more will be, on criteria and guidelines for observing and reporting an election. Some of these are listed to in the bibliography (Appendix 4).

It is acknowledged that there is no generally accepted set of criteria for judging any electoral event. However, priority areas which observers should focus on can be identified. The electoral law and regulations should ensure equitable opportunity for voter participation. The secrecy of the ballot should be assured. Sufficient information should be provided so that electors can make an informed decision. The integrity of voter register should be evident. Sufficient time should be given to political parties to organize and communicate their platforms. The voting and counting processes should be, and should be seen to be, open, honest and free of fraud.

Once the fundamental criteria and priority areas have been defined, they should not be adjusted or made more flexible in order to accommodate specific problems in a given election.

The resultant final observers' report must cover the entire electoral process, from the electoral law through to the proclamation of results, and must take into account the electoral situation and events throughout the entire country.

In some circumstances, a strong argument can be made for the issuing of one or more interim reports prior to polling day or the announcement of results. The number, nature and extent of these interim reports would be influenced by the length of time the observer team was in the country and by the scope of its activities. Certain situations might trigger the desirability for such reports – especially situations where electoral abuse, fraud, intimidation or violence were evident. In these instances, the interim report might focus on observations of only one or two electoral activities, such as voter registration or media bias. Such interim reports can be valuable tools in the hands of electoral authorities before the election, providing them with the opportunity to correct the problems identified. Furthermore, it is often useful to request that the electoral authorities indicate whether corrective action has been taken. If it has and the situation improves, this information should be included in the final report.

Interim reports which identify very critical and deep-seated problems or serious abuses which are not rectified by the election authorities after notification may prompt observers to consider whether they should continue to participate or not. However, withdrawal should be taken only as a last resort following exhaustive efforts to convince the government and the electoral authorities of the need to resolve fundamental problems even if this involves delaying the election date.

Free, Fair, or ??

> The most technically perfect 'free and fair' election counts for nought if democratic government does not eventuate.[2]

The pressures on observers to state categorically whether an election was 'free and fair' can work to their disadvantage because, in most electoral situations, it is difficult to make this kind of absolute determination. Furthermore, in some situations there is blatant and widespread electoral fraud, as occurred in the Philippines in 1987 and in Panama in 1989. In most cases where abuses occur, governments, parties or candidates tend to manipulate the election process more subtly. As a result, observers should make every effort to avoid focusing on the terms 'free and fair', 'bad or good', or other absolute judgements. To reduce media pressure for such evaluations, and to avoid later misunderstandings, observers should inform the media well in advance of polling day of the kind of 'unfair trap' that is caused by 'free and fair' judgements. It is also desirable to avoid other statements which do not capture the essence of the process. If the presentation of a 'free and fair' conclusion is unavoidable, proposed definitions of each of these terms can be found in *A Guide for Election Observers* (Appendix 1).

An election is multi-dimensional, and in reporting on and evaluating this event, it is important to consider each of the major elements of the process and to discuss each one of them in detail, with self-explanatory information. There can be some variations on the theme, but the key elements of any electoral event are essentially as follows:

- Electoral boundaries or districts, and the system of representation;
- Electoral legislation and regulations;
- Voter, party and candidate registration;
- Voter education/voter information;
- The voting and counting process and activities;
- The activities of election officials, the military and the police;
- Media access and freedom of expression;
- The secrecy of the vote;
- Freedom of movement and access;
- Abuse, fraud and intimidation.

Given comprehensive and factual reporting on the above dimensions, the reader should be able to draw his or her own conclusions as to whether the people were fully informed, whether their will was fully and freely expressed, in secret and without fear of intimidation, and whether the whole process was a positive stage in the furtherance of democratic development.

In conclusion, there is a widespread consensus that '... generally, observer groups would do better to be descriptive rather than judgemental'.[3]

Notes

1 *Rights and Responsibilities of Election Observers*, Pierre Cornillon (Secretary General of the Inter-Parliamentary Union). Report presented to the International Conference on *Freedom of Elections and the International Observation of Elections*, La Laguna, Tenerife, 27 February–2 March 1994.

2 The Honourable Clive Griffiths, MLC, February 1994, Wiston House, UK.

3 *The Kenya Election*, Lord Jeffrey Tordoff at the *Conference on Strengthening Democracy*, January 1994, Wiston House, UK.

9 After the Election

Democratic development is seen as the support of good government alongside accountability and competence; it is linked with the protection and promotion of human rights, with respect for the rule of law, for the independence and credibility of the judiciary, and for democratic and responsible government institutions. It is also necessary to have a mechanism in place through which people are periodically consulted and empowered to keep or change their government and to do so in an atmosphere which recognizes key political freedoms, including those of association, assembly and expression.

A democratic culture makes provision for the consultation of the people on a regular basis, be it by the holding of an election, a referendum or a plebiscite. A significant product of this democratic culture is that the results and outcome of these electoral events are then accepted by the public and those involved in the political process in the country. When considering the many different types of electoral systems found in the world, it is important to know if the possibility exists for changing the government by peaceful means. Without this, government lacks legitimacy and accountability.

In his opening remarks to the Conference, Sir Anthony Siaguru, Deputy Secretary-General of the Commonwealth, spoke of the character of democracy as follows:

> One lesson that has been brought home by harsh experience is that democratic government – in its fullest sense – is secure only when it can respond to the deeper values in society, and reflect these in an equitable body of law. There can be no mechanistic translation of institutions: democracy is a complex, multifaceted, open-ended process that requires constant scrutiny so that it does not lose or obscure its most essential elements. More than any other system it is capable of continual renewal, adaptation and regeneration in the face of rapid change and the evolving demands of society. This is its enduring strength.

The Conference generally recognized that the concept of strengthening democracy must look beyond the holding of free and fair elections to the long-term survival of a democratic culture. Democracy requires a healthy environment for its continued growth and survival and for its application in the day-to-day operation of government.

What then contributes to this healthy environment? In his article 'Democracy in the Commonwealth Caribbean', Clifford E. Griffin maintains that four conditions must be present:

> First, a society must be hospitable to the attributes of such a culture. Second, these attributes will take a long time to take root and mature. Third, political and structural conditions must exist to facilitate this maturation. Fourth and finally, a certain level of economic development and resource distribution must be achieved.

He further maintains that:

> ... democratic institutions will flourish in countries with a suitable political culture. Such a culture will develop in a civil society that facilitates the emergence of free associations and institutions distinct from the state. One key factor is a strong legal system. With politics grounded in the rule of law administered by an impartial judicial system, such groups become increasingly confident that they can pursue their varying interests in a democratic environment.

We must also bear in mind that democracy – perhaps especially young democracies – should also deliver results in terms of meeting needs and aspirations. Thus, there is an important link with sound economic policies and expectations. The democratic process depends on the effectiveness of key institutions with complementary, and sometimes counterbalancing, interrelationships. The discussion at the Conference centred around the role of public administration, the judiciary and the military in countries where democratic development is under way.

Since parliaments and legislative bodies at regional and local levels do not always work effectively, there is a need to strengthen parliamentary systems and procedures. Representatives of the parliamentary associations present at the Conference provided information on the role of their associations: they provide training and seminars for newly-elected politicians and for the staff of parliamentary institutions. Parliament must evolve and play an active role in relation to the executive branch, ministers and the public. Networking must be facilitated for key individuals in these organizations, for example the Speaker and the Clerk. It is important to recognize the standing and the vital role that opposition parties play, providing a check on the government and its actions while hopefully supporting the wider framework of institutions within the country.

All in all, these institutions must be accountable to society at large. To accomplish this, the institutions of government need to be open and responsive in style and behaviour; however, to ensure accountability, society needs a voice on a more continuous basis than once every few years. The system must therefore empower the people generally – not just the powerful or the elite, but also the poor and disadvantaged.

The role of the legal system includes resolving disputes and ensuring that the rules of the process are followed; this provides assurance to current government and opposition groups. Less directly but of fundamental importance, the judiciary provides a climate upholding the rule of law – constitutional, criminal, civil and commercial – underpinning not just political but also economic life.

We cannot, however, expect the legal system in young democracies to ensure fairness if it lacks independence and is not perceived to be impartial, if there is a poor legal framework, if corruption is evident or if the system does not have ample resources to function efficiently. Promptness is equally important as fairness or the citizenry may be tempted to pursue less peaceful means for resolving disputes. To improve matters, training could be provided for the judiciary and others in the legal system, assistance given in the review and updating of laws, and external links encouraged for professional support and to help develop or improve systems to provide access to legal protection and redress.

A competent and impartial civil service is needed to ensure the development and administration of government policy and to advise ministers on their powers and limitations. An appropriate relationship is needed between the political and administrative arms of government, to maintain the credibility of, and provide support for, the democratic process as a whole. Government accountability is of great importance; it should make information available through a free media and provide channels through which grievances can be addressed. The competence of individuals within the government and within the civil service is essential, for corruption can easily become endemic.

In order to assist in developing an impartial and efficient public service, exposure could be given to systems of public administration in other countries so that a fixed model is not necessarily promoted. Knowing about alternatives can demonstrate how events are managed differently and how others have solved common problems. Assistance could be furnished to develop and implement programmes aimed at making government more affordable and effective. Once the role of the civil service has been established within the context of a particular country, training in that role and its responsibilities could be provided.

In many countries where democratic development is underway, the role of the military may be an important consideration, especially if the country has had a military form of government or a government backed by the military. According to the general democratic philosophy, the military ought not to have a direct role within government other than ensuring external defence – at the direction of the government. In some cases, funds being expended on the military may drain the budget and retard much needed development and welfare programmes.

Efficient management and democratic accountability of the military is essential. The problem is how to ensure accountability in the democratic context if the military itself has a political role. This situation may require special arrangements for the transition to democracy, keeping in mind the constitutional provisions of the country. Programmes for the demilitarization of the forces and for redefining their role are necessary. It may be possible to assist in this process by providing funds or support for the demilitarization process, for the retraining of demobilized personnel and indirectly by strengthening budgetary and accountability processes.

Supporters of democracy have seen many encouraging developments in recent years, but there have also been setbacks. Reversions to undemocratic governments have shown that there is no straight and easy road to democracy; experiences after some elections have underlined the fact that true democracy is not simply a question of holding an election, however successfully.

As Sir Anthony Siaguru said in his closing remarks: 'The Commonwealth believes in global partnership in advancing the goals of democracy and with this in mind has been establishing closer links with other organizations, both multilateral and bilateral in the field of democratic development.'

The Conference itself provided an important forum for international consensus building and policy development and for collective efforts in advancing the goals of democracy and good governance. Consideration was given to the need to maintain and enhance commitment and vigilance to help nurture and sustain democracy around the world.

10 Conclusion

Over the past several years the major focus for strengthening democracy around the world (other than peacekeeping) has been the holding of elections. However, the international community has learned through bitter experience that, in isolation from other democratic development initiatives, elections are not the complete answer. In the cases of Haiti and Angola, for instance, resources were devoted to elections which were expected to resolve all conflicts. But how could they considering that there was no corresponding attempt to discuss or negotiate underlying deep-seated problems?

Although elections can play a valuable role as a conflict-resolution mechanism, they are dependent for any success in this respect on the establishment of parallel negotiating mechanisms where the parties learn how to solve problems and achieve positive results through discussion and consensus. Examples of elections acting as a conflict-resolution catalyst were dramatically evident in South African recently, and also in Guyana, El Salvador and the Seychelles. In all of the successful cases, there existed conflict-resolution mechanisms other than the elections, including an effective negotiation process through which the parties learned to resolve conflict. The positive experiences gained by the parties in carrying out successful negotiations during the electoral process itself established a solid foundation for strengthening the newly-elected democratic government.

These conflict-resolution mechanisms usually evolve from initiatives of multilateral organizations or outside states who foster and develop them. It is here that organizations such as the Commonwealth Parliamentary Association and the Inter-Parliamentary Union have and should continue to make important and constructive contributions. This is in addition to their participation as technical advisers and observers during elections in their continuing efforts to strengthen democracies around the world.

Appendix 1 A Guide for Election Observers

Introduction

1. Users' Guide

This Reference Guide is designed primarily to assist those election observers:

- who arrive shortly before the polling day(s) and leave soon afterward;
- whose role is to 'passively' evaluate the election, to obtain information concerning electoral activities occurring before their arrival, and to take comprehensive notes of all events during their stay in the country;
- who have not been given authority as 'active' monitors or supervisors to give advice, guidance or instructions to election officials or political representatives, or the mandate to supervise the administration of the election process;
- whose mandate, individually or collectively, is to arrive at a conclusion about the election, based on factual information obtained; and/or
- who report this conclusion publicly to the media, to the responsible organizations of both the host and the sponsoring countries, or who report privately to the sponsoring body.

2. Contents

The Guide is subdivided into six sections:

A. A BASIC APPROACH TO OBSERVING ELECTIONS
B. PRE-ELECTION DAY REVIEW
C. ELECTION DAY: OBSERVING VOTING ACTIVITIES
D. OBSERVING THE COUNTING PROCESS
E. POST-ELECTION DAY CONSIDERATIONS
F. THE OBSERVERS' REPORT(S)

3. Checklists

In addition to the narrative guidelines which follow, a pull-out checklist, located at the back of this Guide, is provided to assist observers when visiting polling stations.

An observers' travel checklist of materials and supplies can also be found at the back of this Guide.

4. Purpose

These guidelines are designed to be general in nature, so as to cover a wide variety of electoral events and systems. As a result, depending on the characteristics of the observer group – including the time and resources available for their preparation, the nature and extent of their observation activities, and the numbers and composition of the group – it may not be possible to follow the guidelines in their entirety, either in sequence or in content. Similarly, observers may not be able to obtain all of the information suggested in this Guide. However, it is important to realize that every insight gained in respect of any of the points outlined here will be of assistance in arriving at the final evaluation.

Readers should be aware that numerous observer guidelines, manuals, checklists and articles on election observing have been prepared by other organizations, which deal in more detail with a number of the subjects in this Guide. Most of these documents can be obtained through the United Nations Electoral Assistance Unit in New York.

The sections which follow have been designed as a general guide. More detailed information can be found in the documents referred to above.

Section A: A Basic Approach to Observing Elections

1. Mandate

Observers will normally be given a mandate by their sponsoring body. As a general rule, they are asked to report on their observations of the election process and to reach conclusions as to whether the election process was administered freely and fairly, and whether the outcome was valid.

To be able to do this, observers must weigh *all* aspects of the electoral process, including what they have experienced on polling day. However, it often happens that observers are not in the country for a long enough period prior to the election to have a comprehensive knowledge and understanding of the electoral environment or the events leading up to election day.

It is therefore invaluable for election observers to seek out those groups which can provide them with comprehensive information that will assist them in meeting their mandate.

2. *Sources of Information*

Observers should attempt to use *all* available briefing sources from both within their own countries and the country whose election is being observed. As much information as possible should be sought before observers visit the polling stations.

Examples of sources can include:

(a) *Foreign affairs departments and diplomatic missions* on the subjects of political and social conditions, medical and security precautions.

(b) *Pre-election advisory, observation or fact-finding teams from the same or other organizations* on the current electoral environment, political and electoral activities, and problems which have occurred.

(c) *Representatives of the responsible electoral body, nationally and locally*, on the Constitution, the Elections Act and Regulations, the electoral organization, election administration and the complaints process.

(d) *Political party representatives* on campaigning, including rallies, the media, registration, violence and intimidation.

(e) *Non-governmental groups* on the human rights situation, voter education and national observer initiatives.

(f) *The 'man-on-the-street'* for his/her views of the election, degree of confidence in the secret ballot and understanding of the choices available.

(g) *The media* on electoral developments, restrictions and activities, intimidation, political bias, etc.

(h) *Pre-election reports and recommendations* made by any of the above groups or organizations.

While making sure that all the subjects listed above are covered as far as is possible, observers should not restrict themselves to the sources mentioned. Rather, they should make use of as many different sources as are available.

Throughout the election, observers will often be the recipients of second or third-hand information and rumours. An objective observer is one who does not accept information at face value **unless** the facts can be verified, preferably first-hand. Observers should remember that the very fact that they are international may add unwarranted credibility to unsubstantiated information that they may mistakenly pass on.

3. Legislation

Although observers are not required to interpret the legislation, it is to their advantage to become familiar with the key elements of the *Constitution, and the Election Law and Regulations*, and how these provide for the essential underpinnings for democratic development through multi-party elections.

Furthermore, an understanding of the legislation will greatly assist in the process of observing the voting and counting, in responding to questions, and in preparing the observers' report(s).

More detailed discussion of the subjects referred to in 1 (Mandate) and 2 (Sources of Information) above will be dealt with in Section B (Pre-Election Day Review).

4. Terms, Conditions and Code of Conduct

Not only may the sponsoring body provide observers with a code of conduct, but some countries may also include a code of conduct for observers in their legislation or regulations. Whether or not a written code of conduct exists, *all* observers should conduct themselves according to the following principles: Observers should:

- obtain official accreditation from the receiving country to permit access to the polls and other election sites;
- be impartial and non-partisan;
- not interfere in the internal jurisdiction or affairs of the country;
- not disrupt or interfere in the election process or at the polls;

- have freedom of access to speak to or meet with all political parties, candidates and election officials, subject to availability;
- have freedom of access to all polls and counting centres at all times, unless they are temporarily overcrowded; and
- have freedom of movement throughout the country, without prior permission or notification, subject to valid security considerations.

5. Recording Observations

In order to facilitate the recording of observations throughout the election period, it is useful to carry a pocket notebook for noting the time, date, place and circumstances observed or complaints received, as these arise.

The very act of taking notes conveys an immediate impression of interest and concern. Where a complaint arises, the recording of the information itself often provides assurance to the complainant that his/her concerns will be conveyed to a higher authority.

Checklists for use both before and on polling day are also helpful reference tools and may be provided by the sponsoring body.

Using notebooks and checklists on the spot will ensure that specific details are easily acccssiblc during the preparation of both the final observation report and of any interim reports, whether planned or required due to special circumstances.

Section B: Pre-Election Day Review

In the previous section, reference was made to potential sources of information which observers might consult prior to visiting the polls.

The following paragraphs focus on the range of topics which might be explored or discussed with the various information sources PRIOR to polling day. These topics include:

1. The Constitution and Election Legislation;
2. Human Rights;
3. The Judiciary;

4. The Military and Police;
5. The Responsible Election Body or Bodies;
6. Electoral Boundaries and Representation;
7. Parties and Candidates;
8. Political Campaigns;
9. The Media;
10. Civic Education and Voter Information;
11. Voter Registration;
12. Voting Procedures;
13. Counting Procedures, and
14. Recounts and Recourse.

Some typical questions or points for consideration on each topic are raised below as a guide to the kind of information which might be sought in the information-gathering phase. There are undoubtedly other questions which observers will wish to add to the list, depending on their particular areas of expertise and concern, as well as on local conditions.

It is essential that observers fully understand the objective of the electoral event, whether it is an election, plebiscite or referendum at the presidential, national and/or local level(s).

1. The Constitution and Election Legislation

Does this legislation provide for:

- basic democratic rights to vote and be elected;
- freedom of speech and expression;
- freedom of assembly and association;
- universal suffrage, and
- the secrecy of the vote?

Are the provisions of the constitution and the electoral legislation being respected and applied systematically and fairly by the government and by the electoral, judicial and other authorities?

Does the electorate perceive that the legislation is applied equitably?

2. *Human Rights*

Are rights such as freedom of expression and assembly respected and applied in an even-handed way?

Is the general population aware of its rights and freedoms?

What are the problems of human rights abuses?

Is there a mechanism for redress?

How quickly are complaints dealt with?

Is the application of human rights principles improving or deteriorating in the period leading up to the election?

3. *The Judiciary*

Is the judiciary independent of political influence?

Is it impartial and does it dispense justice fairly and equitably?

Is it seen to be credible and trusted by the general population?

4. *The Military and Police*

Do the military and the police have significant political influence or exert significant political power?

Do they interfere with civilian control?

Do they play a dominant or influential role in the election process or in government?

Do they intimidate the electorate, parties or candidates by their presence or their actions?

Will they be voting at the regular polls or at special polls?

If at the regular polls, will they be voting in uniform?

Are there, or were there, any states of emergency, curfews or other controls in effect?

5. The Responsible Election Body or Bodies

What is the composition of the senior body?

How and by whom were its members appointed?

Is it independent of government legislatively, structurally, physically and financially?

Does it deal with all political parties in an even-handed way?

Does it apply the electoral act faithfully to the wording and intent of the legislation?

Are the field organizations throughout the country independent and impartial?

Do these offices have the logistical, personnel and material support necessary to carry out their roles and responsibilities?

6. Electoral Boundaries and Representation

What is the representation system – proportional (e.g. the d'Hondt, mixed or other system)? or majoritarian (e.g. first-past-the-post)?

How are the representatives elected or selected (e.g. strict lists, direct voting)?

Are the electoral districts, regions or constituencies defined so as to ensure relatively equal representation of the population?

What were the criteria used in establishing the electoral boundaries; have they been recorded, e.g. in legislation or policy?

Was the establishment of boundaries carried out by a non-partisan independent body?

Is there any evidence of boundaries being drawn to favour one political party over another?

7. Parties and Candidates

How many parties and/or candidates are competing?

How much time was there for new political parties to organize themselves prior to the setting of the election date?

What are the registration/nomination requirements?

Do these discriminate or bar any parties or candidates from competing?

Was the party/candidate registration process conducted fairly?

Is there a code of conduct required of parties/candidates?

Is it respected and followed?

Are any parties boycotting the election?

How are parties funded?

Are there provisions for funding of parties?

Are there limits on contributions or spending by parties and/or candidates?

Is there public reporting (disclosure) of party finances?

Is the political playing field reasonably level?

Is there a clear separation between government activities and resources and those of the governing party?

8. *Political Campaigns*

Are parties/candidates free to conduct political rallies anywhere in the country? Are the financial provisions and constraints concerning campaigning equitable for all parties?

Are permits required to hold meetings?

If so, are they issued equally to all parties?

Has violence or intimidation occurred during the campaign?

How was the violence dealt with by the authorities?

Are there any dispute-resolution mechanisms in place?

Were all parties able to communicate with the electors to the extent and in the manner they wished?

9. *The Media*

Do media services exist that are independent of government control?

Do they present the full range of political views?

Is there any evidence of media control or censorship by the government or any particular party?

Do all parties/candidates have equal access to the media for publicizing their political platforms either in paid or unpaid messages?

Is the media directly or (through other groups) actively involved in voter education?

Does the media have a code of ethics related to the election?

10. Civic Education and Voter Information

What is the nature and scope of the civic education and voter information programme?

What bodies are responsible?

Are the political parties/candidates involved?

Are some programme elements targeted to specific groups such as women, youth, electors with disabilities, aboriginal and ethnic minorities and illiterate electors?

Are the information materials suitable for their target audiences?

Is the electorate adequately informed concerning the democratic process and the range of choices available?

Does the electorate know about the voter registration process and the voting process?

What information materials are available to the electorate?

What is the literacy rate of the country?

If the illiteracy rate is high, what methods are used to disseminate information?

Are these materials produced in the different languages of the electorate (if applicable)?

11. Voter Registration

What are the voter eligibility criteria?

What is the registration process?

Is it necessary to present a voter registration document at the poll?

What is the estimated eligible voter population and on what is this estimate based?

Is the registration undertaken before or during the election period?

How many electors have registered prior to election day?

What percentage of the estimated total does this represent?

How are people's names removed from the register?

How are people added to the register?

What is the deadline for removals or additions?

What provisions are there, if any, for late deletions or additions?

What provisions are there for replacement of lost or stolen registration documents?

What are the most common registration problems?

How do the political parties/candidates view the registration process? Do they play a role in it?

Have some electors not registered and for what reason?

Will the electoral register be up-to-date on polling day?

Is there a mechanism for registration on polling day?

Is there an effective objection and appeal process?

12. Voting Procedures

What is the step-by-step voting procedure?

How many polling stations will there be?

How many electors are expected to use each polling station?

How far will electors have to travel?

What provisions are in place to prevent multiple voting?

What is the nature and extent of the training programme for election officials?

How are the poll officials selected?

Who is permitted to be present in the poll during and outside voting hours?

What is the role of party/candidate agents at the poll?

Are there local and national observers?

What are the special provisions, if any, for prison inmates and handicapped, ill, minority language or illiterate voters?

Are there provisions for voting outside the country?

What are the arrangements for the secure distribution and delivery of election materials and supplies to and from the polls?

To what extent is authority delegated to regional or local poll officials?

What are the telecommunications facilities?

What are the problem-resolution mechanisms established for polling day?

What built-in security measures have been used in printing ballot papers?

How are the ballot boxes sealed?

13. Counting Procedures

Are the ballots to be counted at the polling stations or in one or several central counting centres?

If the ballots are counted at the poll, are the results announced and posted there?

If the count is to be undertaken in a regional counting centre, what are the security arrangements for transporting the ballot boxes and for the duration of the count?

Who will be present when the ballots are counted?

What are the criteria for accepting or rejecting a ballot?

How are the results to be compiled, released and published?

14. Recounts and Recourse

What are the conditions under which recounts may be required?

Who requests them – or are they undertaken automatically under certain circumstances?

Who supervises a recount and declares the final result?

Is there any recourse in the event of a challenged election? Are the courts involved?

15. Pre-Election Activities

Several days to a week before polling day(s), observers should travel to the area(s) they plan to observe in order to locate the polling stations and meet the responsible local election and civic officials. They should discuss with these officials the preparations that are underway for the election and any problems that are being encountered or are anticipated.

It may also be useful to meet local representatives of all political parties as well as other observers. In this way, not only will observers be familiar with the location and with the individuals responsible prior to polling day, but they may also avoid duplication of effort with other observers and will have established an international presence in the community.

Section C: Election Day: Observing Voting Activities

Two options are available to observers visiting polling stations. Ideally, activities should be observed in only one polling station starting before the opening of the polls, throughout the day, till after closing time. (The counting process will be discussed in the next section.) However, because of their limited numbers, most international observers find it preferable to visit a number of polling stations in order to obtain a wider overview of polling day activities, to make some unexpected visits (the surprise element), and to establish an international presence in the region or district, rather than in only one location.

1. Prior to the Opening of the Polling Stations

Observers should arrive at polling stations *prior* to the time scheduled for the opening of the polls. At this time it should be noted whether:

- all required election officials are present;
- all accredited party/candidate representatives are present;
- other national or international observers are present;
- all election supplies and lists of electors are on hand and functional;
- ballots, ballot boxes and seals have been carefully guarded and secured prior and subsequent to their arrival at the poll;
- all forms, protocols and other documents have been signed by those responsible, as required by law;

- the responsible election officials are fully aware of and follow all requirements for setting up and opening the poll;
- ballot boxes are shown to be empty before being sealed in the presence of party/candidate representatives and observers;
- the serial numbers on the ballot boxes, ballot stubs and on the seals used (where applicable) are recorded by those present;
- adequate security for the poll has been provided;
- queues of voters waiting for the polls to open are controlled and orderly; and
- the poll opens on time at the designated hour.

If the poll does not open at the time provided for by law, the reason for the late opening should be recorded.

2. *At the Polling Stations During Voting Hours*

When visiting any polling station, observers should ensure that their activities do not disrupt the voting process in any way. Conversations with election officials should be held only when they are not occupied with voters, and conversations with political/candidates' representatives and other observers should preferably take place outside the polling station. Finally, permission should be obtained from the presiding officer or individual concerned *before* any photographs are taken, as this is frequently discouraged or not permitted.

When inside the polling station, observers should note whether:

- there are long queues of electors and whether these are orderly;
- there is a military or police presence and whether this creates an atmosphere of intimidation;
- there have been any incidents of violence or intimidation at the poll;
- there is any evidence of party or political colours, symbols or propaganda in or near the polling station;
- voters encounter any confusion or difficulty on entering the polling station;
- there are problems related to the list of electors (if applicable) or the acceptability of voter identification documents;

- problems and challenges concerning identity documents, missing documents or voters' lists are expeditiously and knowledgeably dealt with, without seriously disrupting the voting process;
- all procedures related to applying and checking for indelible ink (as applicable) are followed;
- there is sufficient ink and, if related lights or machines are used, whether these are functional;
- the stamping, initialling and issuing of the ballot paper(s) (as applicable) are in accordance with the defined procedures;
- election officials are knowledgeable concerning special provisions (if any) which might apply to blind, disabled, illiterate or other electors who may need extra assistance;
- to what extent voting by blind, disabled or illiterate voters is a secret vote and whether this group forms a significant percentage of the population;
- on leaving the voting screen, voters have folded their ballots so as to ensure the secrecy of their choice;
- election officials ensure that all ballots cast are deposited in the correct ballot box;
- electors leave the polls in a quiet and orderly manner;
- political party representatives are able to witness and, if necessary, question or challenge any aspect of the voting process; and
- the administration of the polls is such as to create confidence that all electors will be able to cast their votes within the time allotted.

Observers may find it useful to determine the average time it takes an individual to vote from entry to departure. In addition, depending on what time of day their visit takes place, observers may be able to forecast (by estimating the proportion of votes already cast, the time remaining, the number of people waiting and the average time to process each elector) whether all electors will be able to vote before the official close of the polls. In some cases, where it appears there may be problems in this respect, observers may wish to revisit certain polls.

3. The Closing of the Poll

Observers should attempt to attend the closing of those polls where problems were anticipated, such as queues of electors still waiting to vote.

At the close of the polls, observers should determine whether:

- the polls closed at the time provided for by law;
- the closing of the poll was extended due to late opening or other similar circumstances (as provided by law or at the personal discretion of the election official);
- electors who had not yet voted but were 'in line' were permitted to vote (as provided for in the law or at the personal discretion of the election official);
- there were any disruptive or violent incidents related to the closing of the poll;
- all procedures and reports related to the closing of the poll were followed;
- all necessary security provisions concerning ballots, ballot stubs, ballot boxes, seals, etc. were respected; and
- party/candidate agents and observers were satisfied with the actions taken by the poll official(s).

Section D: Observing the Counting Process

The counting of the ballots is often carried out at the polling stations immediately after the close of the polls. For security reasons, however, some countries conduct the counting at one central location or at a number of regional counting centres. In these situations, ballot boxes and related materials need to be transported, thereby raising additional concerns which the observer must take into account.

1. Transportation of Ballots from the Polling Station to a Counting Centre

Where ballots are transported from the polling station to a counting centre, observers should determine whether:

- all the ballot boxes, seals, unused ballots, stubs, etc. being sent have been properly sealed, secured and recorded;
- all the preparations have been observed by party/candidate agents and observers;
- the responsible election officials, military or police, as determined by the election authorities, are present and have provided suitable transportation facilities and adequate security;
- the ballot boxes, related election materials and reports are accompanied *in the same vehicle* by party/candidate agents and possibly by observers;
- the length of time taken to transport the ballot boxes from the poll to the counting centre is unreasonably long;
- there were any incidents or complaints relating to the transport of ballot boxes; and
- on arrival, there is any evidence of tampering with or the replacement of any of the balloting materials.

2. *Counting at the Poll or Counting Centre*

At the poll or counting centre, the observer should determine whether:

- party/candidate agents and observers are present throughout;
- media representatives are permitted;
- security is adequate and is the responsibility of the military or the police;
- counting officials are well-trained and fully aware of all the steps required;
- ballot boxes are unsealed in the presence of agents and observers;
- the ballots in each box are totalled separately;
- the total number of ballots in the box is reconciled with the total number of ballot stubs (less spoiled ballots) and with the number of electors who voted (depending on the electoral system);
- any irregularities were noted before mixing the ballots with those of any other boxes and/or starting the count (depending on the electoral system);

- all sorting and counting of ballots were open and clearly visible to agents and observers;
- decisions as to rejected or invalid ballots were consistent, equitable and in accordance with the law;
- the number of invalid ballots was significant enough to suggest a protest vote or a lack of knowledge as to how to mark the ballot by the elector;
- party/candidate agents challenged counting or invalid ballot decisions and whether these were dealt with in accordance with the law;
- party/candidate agents and observers were permitted to make or were given copies of the results of the count(s) which they observed;
- the result was announced at the counting site or forwarded to a higher authority for announcement;
- a parallel 'quick count' was carried out by observer groups;
- following completion of the count, all balloting materials were secured and guarded; and
- balloting materials were sent to another location for recount or storage and, if so, were accompanied by agents and/or observers.

Section E: Post-Election Day Considerations

It is quite common to find that even unofficial election results are not available on election night. In such cases, partial results may not be sufficient to predict the final outcome. In some instances, several days or even weeks are required before the official results are announced. Because the greater the length of time that elapses between the count and the announcement of the results, the greater the level of suspicion and accusations of manipulation and fraud, this period presents a critical challenge to observers.

Observers should therefore attempt to follow closely all final vote tallying which may take place in the period leading up to the announcement of the official results.

Once the announcement is made, the observers should:

- determine the levels of credibility and of public acceptance given to the announcement;

- determine the percentage of votes cast in relation to the total number of electors to establish whether a majority of the population voted;
- calculate the total number and percentage of spoiled and rejected (invalid) ballots to establish whether these had any significant impact on the results. If so, an attempt should be made to determine the cause of this occurrence;
- determine the number and percentage of votes and seats obtained by parties/candidates and assess the overall results, thus establishing whether those results indicate a clear, unqualified expression of the wishes of the electorate;
- try to establish whether all participating parties accepted the results and the seriousness of any complaints or objections; and
- determine how expeditiously investigations and complaints were handled and by what authority.

Given the importance of these factors, it is desirable that at least some observers remain for a reasonable period after polling day in order to obtain first-hand information to complete their reports.

Section F: The Observers' Report(s)

Observers may be asked to make one (or more) of the following types of reports:

1. 'Off-the-cuff' Reports

An informal, on-the-spot 'report' is sometimes requested by the media, by an embassy, by political or electoral officials or others during the course of the election. In such circumstances, observers are advised to provide very little or no information, rather than comment, perhaps unwisely, on electoral processes which are not yet complete, or risk compromising their impartial status by making premature judgements.

2. Special Reports

A special report may be made during the electoral period preceding polling day. There may be one or a series of these reports. They could be status reports on the progress of the various electoral activities or they could focus on specific problems, abuses or other negative situations which may be expected to have a detrimental impact on the election. These types of reports are sometimes useful as a basis for discussions with election, government or party officials in order to resolve problems as and when they are identified. Although such reports are often produced by pre-election monitoring or technical assistance teams, it may sometimes be desirable and useful for observers to prepare one or more interim report(s).

3. The Observer's Report

During the course of the election, members of observation teams will often visit different polling stations and will record their comments separately. Subsequently these observations will be discussed and amalgamated into an observers' group report. The comments and suggestions which follow provide some guidelines as to the context and approach to the preparation of this final report of the observer team. (A single observer who is not part of a team should also use the guidelines which follow in preparing his or her final report.)

4. The Observer Team Report

(a) Deciding on Contents This report should identify the participants of the observer group and briefly describe their activities from the time of arrival to the time of departure. The sources of their information, especially with respect to events which occurred prior to their arrival or which they did not observe first-hand, should be reported.

It is usually helpful to review the 14 areas described in Section B of this Guide (Pre-Election Day Review), and to report on any critical matters – positive or negative – especially those which had a lasting influence on the electoral event.

This can be followed by a description of the group's observation of the voting activities on polling day, including the count. Examples of significant observations made by members should be provided.

(b) Drawing Conclusions This narrative review of the electoral process will in itself often lead to an obvious conclusion as to the group's overall evaluation of the electoral event. While every election has its flaws and problems, in the majority of cases these are not sufficient grounds to reject the whole process. However, there have been instances where elections were clearly illegitimate. The most difficult evaluations to make involve those elections which fall somewhere between the two extremes. In such

cases, the job of the observer is often made even harder by pressures from the media and others to render an *absolute* judgement as to whether the election was 'free and fair'.

(c) Was the Election 'Free and Fair'? At the outset, observers should avoid the 'trap' of evaluating an electoral event as free and fair on the grounds that all aspects of the voting process went smoothly on polling day, with no evidence of major incidents of fraud, intimidation or disruption. Indeed, before deciding whether an election has been free and fair, a smooth-running polling day must be viewed in the context of the legislative and political environment and of the events preceding as well as following polling day, up to and including the announcement of the official results.

Definitions — In reviewing all of these elements in the context of 'free' and 'fair' elections, the following definitions are offered for consideration:

'FREE' = an electoral process where fundamental human rights and freedoms are respected, including:

- freedom of speech and expression by electors, parties, candidates and the media;
- freedom of association; that is, freedom to form organizations such as political parties and NGOs;
- freedom of assembly, to hold political rallies and to campaign;
- freedom of access to and by the elector to transmit and receive political and electoral information messages;
- freedom to register as an elector, as a party or as a candidate;
- freedom from violence, intimidation or coercion;
- freedom of access to the polls by electors, party agents and accredited observers;
- freedom to exercise the franchise in secret; and
- freedom to question, challenge and register complaints or objections without negative repercussions.

'FAIR' = an electoral process where the 'playing field' is reasonably level and accessible to all electors, parties and candidates. This includes:

- an independent, non-partisan electoral organization to administer the process;
- guaranteed rights and protection through the constitution and electoral legislation and regulations;
- equitable representation of electors provided through legislation;
- clearly-defined universal suffrage and secrecy of the vote;
- equitable criteria and opportunities to register as an elector, a political party or a candidate;
- equitable and balanced reporting by the media;
- equitable access to financial and material resources for party and candidate campaigning;
- equitable opportunities for the electorate to receive political and voter information;
- accessible polling places;
- equitable treatment of electors, candidates and parties by election officials, the government, the police, the military and the judiciary;
- an open and transparent ballot-counting process, and
- an election process which is not disrupted by violence, intimidation or coercion.

(d) Conclusion Since no electoral event can be considered flawless in terms of the above criteria, the degree of impact of any positive or negative events must be assessed with the following question in mind: **was the will of the majority of the voters expressed freely, clearly and knowledgeably, and in secret?**

Therefore, when determining whether an election was 'free and fair', the observer should avoid being pressured into making a judgement in absolute terms. To arrive at a conclusion in this respect, after taking all observations into account, observers should ask themselves **to what degree** the election was free and fair, and **to what extent** the election made a significant and positive contribution to the democratic evolution or development of the country concerned.

The final evaluation should normally be determined by all observer group members – *by consensus* – following a review of the factual information gathered.

Polling Day Checklist for Observers

The 'yes', 'no', numerical or other summary entries on this checklist should be supplemented on each day of voting by a narrative description (by poll and item numbers) of your observations.

No.	Subject of Observation	Poll#	Poll#	Poll#	Poll#
1	What was the time of observers' arrival?				
2	What was the time of observers' departure?				
The Polling Place					
3	Was the poll suitable (location, access, security, flow, crowd control, space)?				
4	If this was a multiple polling site, how many polls did it contain?				
5	Were there complaints about the poll location?				
6	Were all required polling officials present?				
7	Were party or candidates' agents present?				
8	Was there any evidence of problems or conflict among party agents?				

No.	Subject of Observation	Poll#	Poll#	Poll#	Poll#
9	Were observers (national, international) present?				
10	Was there a presence (in or outside the poll) of military or police?				
11	Were armed security forces inside the polls?				
12	Was a supervising official readily available to resolve problems?				
13	Did polling officials have a good understanding of their responsibilities?				
14	At what time did the poll open (on time, late)?				
15	Were ballot boxes shown to be empty before being sealed at the opening of the poll?				
16	Were ballot boxes sealed securely with numbered seals?				
17	Did party agents and observers record the ballot box and ballot seal numbers?				
18	Were there any partisan signs or materials in the poll?				
19	Was there any evidence of campaigning in or near the polls?				
20	Did electors have any problems finding the correct voting line or table?				

No.	Subject of Observation	Poll#	Poll#	Poll#	Poll#
21	Were all polling supplies on hand before opening?				
22	Were any voters armed in the polling station?				
The Voting Process					
23	Were any problems encountered with voters' lists/register of electors?				
24	Were there any problems with voters' identification documents?				
25	Were list and identity card problems resolved quickly?				
26	Were electors' hands checked for ink?				
27	Was ink applied to all electors' hands?				
28	Were there any problems with the inking process?				
29	Was the voting process clearly explained to electors?				
30	Were all ballots handled identically when given to electors?				
31	Were ballots stamped or initialled by the polling official?				
32	Did the military/police vote at the poll?				
33	Did the military/police vote in uniform?				

No.	Subject of Observation	Poll#	Poll#	Poll#	Poll#
34	Could blind persons vote secretly?				
35	Could illiterate persons vote secretly?				
36	Were there large numbers of illiterate voters?				
37	Could any ballot be linked to a specific elector?				
38	Did the voting compartment location provide for secrecy?				
39	Did electors have difficulty in voting?				
40	Were most electors familiar with the voting process?				
41	What proportion of electors took a long period of time to mark their ballots (indicating problems with comprehension)?				
42	Were ballots folded to ensure secrecy after voting?				
43	What was the average waiting time to vote?				
44	How long did it take to vote from entry to exit?				
45	Did electors seem to be voting of their own free will?				
46	Did electors believe their vote was secret?				
47	Did any queuing electors give up and leave before voting? (how many?)				

No.	Subject of Observation	Poll#	Poll#	Poll#	Poll#
48	Was transportation available for electors?				
49	What was the maximum number of electors planned for at this poll?				
50	How many electors voted?				
Closing of the Poll					
51	At what time did the poll close (on time, late)?				
52	How many people were waiting to vote at closing?				
53	Was voting continued after closing?				
54	Was there any evidence of conflict or violence?				
55	Were there complaints about the voting process?				
56	When the polls closed, were the required reports completed?				
The Count					
57	Was counting carried out at the poll?				
58	How soon after the poll closing did counting commence?				
59	If boxes and supplies were transported to a counting site, were they secure en route?				

No.	Subject of Observation	Poll#	Poll#	Poll#	Poll#
60	Were all materials accompanied by two or more agents from different parties?				
61	On arrival, were all boxes and seals carefully checked and observed?				
62	Before counting started, was a reconciliation made between the number of voters, ballot stubs and spoiled ballots, and the number of ballots in the box?				
63	Were reconciliation problems resolved before counting?				
64	Were party agents and observers present for the count?				
65	Were the counting officials knowledgeable about the process?				
66	Were counting disputes resolved promptly?				
67	Did all officials and party agents sign a copy of the record of the count?				
68	Did agents and observers receive a copy of the record?				
69	How long did it take to complete the count?				
70	Following the count, were the results publicly announced by election officials?				

No.	Subject of Observation	Poll#	Poll#	Poll#	Poll#
71	Were the ballots and other election documents secured and sealed after the count?				
72	If ballots and election documents were sent to another location, were security provisions adequate?				
73	Were ballots accompanied by two or more agents from different parties?				
74	Were there challenges, complaints or discussions about the counting process?				
75	Were these resolved satisfactorily?				

Observers' Travel Checklist of Materials and Supplies

Note: Many of these items may not be required depending on the nature, length and location of the assignment. Conversely, other items not on this list may be required or desirable. In any event, take only the minimum number of items required and, wherever possible, take wash-and-wear clothing. Avoid taking expensive watches or jewellery.

Required for this trip (*)	Item	Quantity Packed or Amount ( )
	Adapter – converter and plugs – 220v to 110v	
	Airline tickets	
	Alarm clock	
	Bathing suit	
	Belly-bag	
	Belt	
	Binoculars	
	Blouses – Shirts –T Shirts	
	Books – Magazines	

Required for this trip (*)	Item	Quantity Packed or Amount ( )
	Bottle opener – corkscrew	
	Bottled water or water-purifying tablets	
	Briefing material	
	Calculator – extra batteries	
	Candles	
	Camera and Film	
	Coat – Raincoat, Wind breaker, Anorak	
	Computer citizenship card	
	Credit cards	
	Currency (cash)	
	Dictating machine	
	Discs	
	Dresses	
	Extra bag (folding)	
	Extra plastic bags for laundry, etc.	
	Flashlight – extra batteries	
	Glasses (and an extra pair)	
	Gloves	
	Hairdryer	
	Handkerchiefs	
	Hat	

Required for this trip (*)	Item	Quantity Packed or Amount ( )
	Insecticide	
	Iron	
	Itinerary	
	Laundry items – Soap – Travel clothes line	
	Locks and keys for baggage and extras	
	Luggage cart	
	Matches	
	Medical supplies: required pills, aspirin, bandaids, etc.	
	Moneybelt	
	Mosquito net	
	Office material – map	
	Out-of-country insurance	
	Pants, slacks, skirts, shorts	
	Passport and photocopies of pages 2 and 3	
	Passport photos (carry 4 to 6 spare)	
	Pens, pencils, paper, notebook, paper clips, scotch tape	
	Pillow – inflatable	
	Pocket knife	
	Purse	

Required for this trip (*)	Item	Quantity Packed or Amount ( )
	Radio – short wave – extra batteries	
	Razor – shaver	
	Rope	
	Rubber boots	
	Scarf	
	Shoes – dress, running shoes, sandals	
	Socks – stockings – pantyhose	
	Suits	
	Suntan lotion (#15 plus)	
	Sunglasses	
	Sweaters	
	Tape – masking, packaging, cellophane tape	
	Tapes for dictating machine	
	Ties	
	Toilet paper	
	Toiletries: soap, shampoo, makeup, brush, comb, toothbrush, toothpaste, sanitary napkins, etc.	
	Towel – Washcloth	
	Travellers cheques (including small denominations)	
	Umbrella	

Required for this trip (*)	**Item**	**Quantity Packed or Amount ( )**
	Underwear	
	Vaccination book	
	Visa	
	Wet napkins – Packaged hand wipes	

Appendix 2 List of Conference Participants

ABRAHAMSEN, Joergen	DENMARK Minister Counsellor, Ministry of Foreign Affairs, Copenhagen
AL-SHAIJI, Abdullah	KUWAIT Professor, Political Science Faculty, Kuwait University
ARTHUR, Owen	BARBADOS Leader of the Opposition, Bridgetown
BAILIE, Warren	CANADA Chief Election Officer of Ontario; Commissioner, Election Finances Act and Officer of the Legislative Assembly, Ontario
BECH, Jon	NORWAY Minister, Royal Norwegian Embassy, London
BONEO, Horacio (Speaker)	UNITED NATIONS Head, UN Electoral Assistance Unit, Department of Political Affairs, United Nations, New York
BOYER, Patrick (Speaker) Mrs Corinne BOYER	CANADA Former Member, House of Commons, Ottawa
BROAD, David	UNITED KINGDOM Head of Commonwealth Coordination Department, Foreign and Commonwealth Office, London

BUCKNELL, Bruce	UNITED KINGDOM Policy Coordinator, Africa Command, Foreign and Commonwealth Office, London
CAIRNCROSS, David	UNITED KINGDOM Associate Director, Wilton Park, Steyning
Baroness CHALKER OF WALLASEY (Visiting Speaker)	UNITED KINGDOM Minister of State for Foreign and Commonwealth Affairs and Minister for Overseas Development, London
CHARBONNEAU, Michel (Speaker)	CANADA Substitute President, Quebec Branch, International Assembly of French-Speaking Parliamentarians (AIPLF)
CLWYD, Ann (Visiting Speaker)	UNITED KINGDOM Labour Member for Cynon Valley, House of Commons, London
DONAHOE, Arthur (Co-Chairman and Speaker)	COMMONWEALTH PARLIAMENTARY ASSOCIATION Secretary-General, Commonwealth Parliamentary Association, London; Canadian national
ELIADES, Demetris (Speaker)	CYPRUS Member of Parliament, Nicosia; Practising Lawyer
ERNESTA, Dolor	SEYCHELLES Minister of Community Development, Seychelle Islands
FERGUS, Hon Howard (Speaker)	MONTSERRAT Speaker of the Legislative Council, Montserrat; School of Continuing Studies, University of the West Indies, Montserrat

GARDNER, Charmaine (Speaker)	ST LUCIA Deputy President of the Senate, Castries, St Lucia
GILANI, Hon Yusuf Raza Mrs GILANI	PAKISTAN Speaker of the National Assembly, Islamabad
GOMEZ, Raja	COMMONWEALTH PARLIAMENTARY ASSOCIATION Director of Administration, Commonwealth Parliamentary Association Secretariat, London; Sri Lanka national
GOODENOUGH, Anthony (Session Participant)	UNITED KINGDOM Assistant Under-Secretary of State for Africa, Foreign and Commonwealth Office, London
GOULD, Ronald (Rapporteur)	CANADA Assistant Chief Electoral Officer for Canada, Ottawa
GRIFFITHS, Hon Clive (Speaker)	AUSTRALIA President, Legislative Council, Parliament of Western Australia; MP for the South Metropolitan Region of Western Australia
HARTLAND, John	COUNCIL OF EUROPE Counsellor, Office of the President, Council of Europe, Strasbourg
HOPKINSON, Nicholas (Deputy Chairman)	UNITED KINGDOM Senior Associate Director, Wilton Park, Steyning
IMLACH, Andrew	COMMONWEALTH PARLIAMENTARY ASSOCIATION Editor of Publications, Commonwealth Parliamentary Association Secretariat, London; Canadian national

JACKSON, Christine (Assistant Rapporteur)	CANADA Electoral Officer, Elections Canada, Ontario
JASKIERNIA, Jerzy (Speaker)	POLAND Chairman of the Legislative Committee of the SEJM, Warsaw
JONES, Sonia	JAMAICA Lawyer; Human Rights Advocate, Kingston
KEATLEY, Patrick (Speaker)	UK/CANADA President, UK Branch, Commonwealth Journalists Association, London
KOEHLER, Michael	GERMANY Cabinet of the Minister for Economic Cooperation and Development, Bonn
LANGHORNE, Richard (Co-Chairman)	UNITED KINGDOM Director, Wilton Park and Wiston House Conference Centre, Steyning
LAU, Teik Soon	SINGAPORE Member of Parliament; Department of Political Science, National University of Singapore
LUCAS, Joycelyn	TRINIDAD AND TOBAGO Chief Election Officer, Elections and Boundaries Commission, Port-of-Spain
MARSHALL, Sir Michael (Visiting Speaker)	UNITED KINGDOM President, Inter-Parliamentary Council, Inter-Parliamentary Union; Conservative Member for Arundel, House of Commons, London

MERLOE, Patrick (Speaker)	UNITED STATES OF AMERICA Senior Associate for Election Processes, National Democratic Institute for International Affairs, Washington, DC
MIRDHA, Hon Ram Niwas (Speaker)	INDIA Member of Parliament (Lok Sarha); Mernber, Executive Committee of Commonwealth Parliamentary Association
MITCHELL, Fred	BAHAMAS Senator, People's Democratic Force, Nassau
MOHAMED, Hon Mohamed Haniffa	SRI LANKA Member of Parliament; Hon Speaker of Sri Lanka
MORKEL, Somerset	SOUTH AFRICA Counsellor (Press), South African Embassy, London
MORPHET, Sally	UNITED KINGDOM Head, International Section, Research and Analysis Department, Foreign and Commonwealth Office, London
MORRIS, Robert	BARBADOS Member of Parliament; Deputy General Secretary, Barbados Workers' Union
MWIINGA, Hon Bennie (Speaker)	ZAMBIA Minister for Local Government and Housing, Lusaka
NDLOVU, Johnson (Speaker)	ZIMBABWE Member of Parliament, Harare

PAROZ, Jean-François	SWITZERLAND Political Division (Latin America, Eastern and Western Africa), Federal Department of Foreign Affairs, Berne
PINTO-DUSCHINSKY, Michael	UNITED KINGDOM Governor, Westminster Foundation for Democracy, London; Pembroke College, Oxford
RANA, Pashupati (Speaker)	NEPAL Secretary-General, National Democratic Party, Kathmandu
REYNOLDS, Diana	COMMONWEALTH PARLIAMENTARY ASSOCIATION Assistant Editor/Information Officer, Commonwealth Parliamentary Association Secretariat, London; UK national
von ROTTENBURG, Fritz	GERMANY Minister/Counsellor; Head, Division for Third World Policy, Democratization and Aid, Federal Ministry of Foreign Affairs, Bonn
RUHEE, Hon Keertee	MAURITIUS Minister for Civil Service Affairs and Employment, Port Louis
SÄVE-SÖDERBERGH, Bengt (Visiting Speaker)	SWEDEN Ambassador, Ministry of Foreign Affairs; Chairman, International Electoral Institute Commission, Stockholm
SELEPENG, Molosiwa	BOTSWANA Permanent Secretary (Political Affairs), Office of the President, Republic of Botswana, Gaborone

SHEPHERD, Colin (Speaker)	UNITED KINGDOM Chairman, Executive Committee of Commonwealth Parliamentary Association; Conservative Member for Hereford, House of Commons
SIAGURU, Sir Anthony (Visiting Speaker)	COMMONWEALTH SECRETARIAT Deputy Secretary-General, Commonwealth Secretariat, London; Papua New Guinea national
SIMONOV, Alexei (Speaker)	RUSSIA Journalist; Chairman, Glastnost Defence Foundation, Moscow
SORENSEN, Jens Adser	DENMARK Head of International Department, Folketinget, Copenhagen
SPARKHALL, Kevin	UNITED KINGDOM Principal Government and Institutions Adviser, Overseas Development Administration (ODA), London
SSEMOGERERE, Hon Paul (Speaker)	UGANDA Second Deputy Prime Minister and Minister of Foreign Affairs, Kampala
STAVAAS, Pia	SWEDEN Lawyer; First Secretary, Department for International Development Cooperation, Ministry for Foreign Affairs, Stockholm
TORDOFF, Lord (Visiting Speaker)	UNITED KINGDOM Chief Liberal Democrat Whip, House of Lords, London
TOVUA, Hon Paul	SOLOMON ISLANDS Speaker of the National Parliament, Honiara

TUUNANEN, Heikki	FINLAND Director in Department for Development Cooperation, FINNIDA, Ministry for Foreign Affairs, Helsinki
WARWICK, Diana	UNITED KINGDOM Chief Executive, Westminster Foundation for Democracy, London
WELLS, Loren (Lorie) (Speaker/Assistant Rapporteur)	CANADA Assistant Chief Election Officer (Acting), Elections Ontario, Scarborough
WENBAN-SMITH, Nigel	UNITED KINGDOM Retired Diplomat; Secretary of the Commonwealth Magistrates and Judges Association, London
ZIEGELER, Holger	GERMANY Assistant Head, Public Relations Division, Federal Ministry of Foreign Affairs, Bonn

Appendix 3 Conference Programme and Presenters

Presentations

The Importance of Free and Fair Elections to Good Governance

Sir Anthony Siaguru
Deputy Secretary-General, Commonwealth Secretariat, London

The Role of Constitutions, Referenda and Constituent Assemblies in Producing an Acceptable Political System

Patrick Boyer, QC
Former Member, House of Commons, Ottawa

Do Elections Exacerbate Ethnic and Regional Tensions?

The Hon Dr Paul Ssemogerere
Second Deputy Prime Minister and Minister of Foreign Affairs, Kampala

Is There a Role for Non-Geographical Constituencies and Nominated Members in Ensuring the Representation of Minority, Aboriginal and Regional Groups?

The Hon Dr Howard Fergus
Speaker of the Legislative Council, Montserrat

Building Civil Society: Voter Education and Strengthening Democratic Political Parties

Johnson Ndlovu, MP
Zimbabwe *and*
Demetris Eliades, MP
Cyprus

Approaches to Election Monitoring

Dr Horacio Boneo
Head, Electoral Assistance Unit, Department of Political Affairs
United Nations, New York *and*
Patrick Merloe
Senior Associate for Election Processes, National Democratic Institute for International Affairs, Washington, DC

Facilitating the Proper Functioning of Parliament: The Role of the Commonwealth Parliamentary Association and Other Parliamentary Associations

Arthur Donahoe, QC
Secretary-General, Commonwealth Parliamentary Association
London *and*
Sir Michael Marshall, MP
President, Inter-Parliamentary Council, Inter-Parliamentary Union and Conservative Member for Arundel, House of Commons, London
and
Michel Charbonneau
Substitute President
Assemblée internationale des parlementaires (AIPLF)
Québec Branch

The Media and Elections: Ensuring Equal Access and Responsible Reporting

Patrick Keatley
President, Commonwealth Journalists Association
London *and*
Colin Shepherd, MP
Chairman, Executive Committee of the Commonwealth Parliamentary Association and Conservative Member for Hereford, House of Commons
London

After the Election: The Role of the Judiciary, Public Administration and the Military in Guaranteeing Good Government

The Rt Hon the Baroness Chalker of Wallasey
Minister of State for Foreign and Commonwealth Affairs and Minister for Overseas Development
London

What is a Free and Fair Election? What are the Mechanisms for Redress of Grievances and the Role of Monitors in Reporting an Unsatisfactory Result?

The Hon Clive Griffiths, MLC
President of the Legislative Council
Western Australia

The Case for an International Institute for Electoral Cooperation and Assistance

Ambassador Bengt Säve-Söderbergh
Chairman, International Electoral Institute Commission
Stockholm

Discussion Groups

Preparing the Electoral Ground

a. *The Work of the Boundary Commission in Ensuring Accessibility, Regularity and Consistency*
The Hon Ram Niwas Mirdha, MP
India

b. *Agreeing a Representative Electoral Roll*
Loren Wells
Assistant Chief Election Officer (Acting)
Elections Ontario, Scarborough

c. *Selection and Financing of Candidates*
Ann Clwyd, MP
Labour Member for Cynon Valley, House of Commons, London

Case Studies of Elections

a. *Kenya*
Lord Tordoff
Chief Liberal Democrat Whip
House of Lords, London

b. *Guyana*
Senator Charmaine Gardner
Deputy President of the Senate
Castries, St. Lucia

c. *Nepal*
Pashupati Rana
Secretary-General, National Democratic Party
Kathmandu

d. *Poland*
Dr Jerzy Jaskiernia
Chairman, Legislative Committee of the Sejm and
Member of Parliament for the Democratic Left, Warsaw

e. *Russia*
Alexei Simonov
Journalist and Chairman, Glasnost Defence Foundation
Moscow

Appendix 4 Bibliography

Boyer, J. Patrick, M.A., LL.B. (1981) *Political Rights: The Legal Framework of Elections in Canada*, Butterworths: Toronto.

Boyer, J. (1992) 'Is a Mandate from the People on Fundamental Issues Essential to a Healthy Democracy?', *Parliamentary Government* (June), no. 41, pp. 3–17.

Canada (1991) Royal Commission on Electoral Reform and Party Financing, *Research Studies*, Dundurn Press: Toronto.

Volume 7, *Ethno-Cultural Groups and Visible Minorities in Canadian Politics*, ed. Kathy Megyery.

Volume 9, *Aboriginal Peoples and Electoral Reform in Canada*, ed. Robert A. Milen.

Volume 10, *Democratic Rights and Electoral Reform in Canada*, ed. Michael Cassidy.

Volume 21, *Election Broadcasting in Canada*, ed. Frederick J. Fletcher.

Canada (1994) 'Report of the Broadcasting Arbitrator, 1993' in *Towards the 35th General Election: Report of the Chief Electoral Officer of Canada*, Ottawa.

Canada (1994) Royal Commission on Electoral Reform and Party Financing (1991) *Reforming Electoral Democracy: Final Report*, Ottawa.

Cornillon, Pierre, 1994 *Rights and Responsibilities of Election Observers*, Report presented by the Secretary-General of the Inter-Parliamentary Union to the International Conference on *Freedom of Elections and the International Observation of Elections*, La Laguna, Tenerife, 27 February–2 March 1994.

Corry, J.A. (1951) *Democratic Government and Politics*, 2nd edn. (revised and enlarged), University of Toronto Press: Toronto.

Dundas, Carl (1993) *Organizing Free and Fair Elections at Cost-Effective Levels*, Technical Assistance Group, Commonwealth Fund for Technical Cooperation, Commonwealth Secretariat: London.

Ewing, Keith D. (1992) *Money, Politics and Law: A Study of Electoral Campaign Finance Reform in Canada*, Clarendon Press: Oxford.

Garber, Larry, ed. (1984) *Guidelines for International Election Observing* (3rd printing, 1990), The International Human Rights Law Group: Washington, DC.

Goodwin-Gill, Guy S. (1994) *Free and Fair Elections: International Law and Practice*, Inter-Parliamentary Union: Geneva.

Griffin, Clifford E. (1993) 'Democracy in the Commonwealth Caribbean', *Journal of Democracy* (April), vol. 4, no. 2, pp. 84–94.

Horowitz, David (1993) 'Democracy in Divided Societies', *Journal of Democracy* (October), vol. 4, no. 4, pp. 18–38.

Journal of Democracy (1993) 'The Challenge of Ethnic Conflict' (A series of case studies: Nigeria, India, Canada, Eastern Europe, Balkans) (October), vol. 4, no. 4, pp. 39–103.

Lakeman, Enid (1982) *Power to Elect: The Case for Proportional Representation*, Heinemann: London.

Linton, Martin (1994) *Money and Votes*, Institute for Public Policy Research: London.

Merloe, Patrick (1993) *Election Campaign Broadcasting in Transitional Democracies: Problems, Principles and Guidelines*, Article 19, International Centre Against Censorship: London.

Merloe, Patrick (1994) *Monitoring Media Fairness in Election Campaigns: An Introduction to Basic Issues*, National Democratic Institute for International Affairs: Washington, D C.

Reeve, Andrew and Ware, Alan (1992) *Electoral Systems: A Comparative and Theoretical Introduction*, Routledge: London.

Steed, Michael (1985) 'The Constituency', in J. Paul Johnson and Harvey E. Pasis eds. (1990) *Representation and Electoral Systems*, Prentice-Hall Canada: Scarborough, Ontario.

Sweden, The International Electoral Institute Commission (1993), *Free and Fair Elections and Beyond, Final Report*, Ministry for Foreign Affairs: Stockholm.

Tordoff, Jeffrey, 'The Kenya Election', presented at the *Conference on Strengthening Democracy*, Wiston House, UK, 31 January–4 February 1994.

Vengroff, Richard (1994) 'The Impact of the Electoral System on the Transition to Democracy in Africa: The Case of Mali', *Electoral Studies* (March), vol. 13, no. 1, pp. 29–37.

Appendix 5 Electoral Law and Practice Report of the CPA Study Group

Chairman: Mr Patrick Boyer, MP, *Canada*
Rapporteur: Mr Jean-Marc Hamel, *Chief Electoral Officer, Canada*

The rules, regulations and procedures governing the conduct of elections, one of the most basic activities in parliamentary democracy, were the subject of three days of discussions by seven Commonwealth Members of Parliament at a special study group meeting held from 25 to 27 September 1985 in Halifax, Nova Scotia, Canada. Held under the auspices of the Commonwealth Parliamentary Association, this Study Group produced the following Report on the laws and practices which determine how political power will be acquired and lost. The Report was then discussed at the 31st Commonwealth Parliamentary Conference and, briefly, at the Fifth Commonwealth Parliamentary Conference of Members from Small Countries, both held a few days later in Saskatchewan, Canada. A summary of those conference discussions follows the Report.

Preface

This Study Group on 'Electoral Law and Practice', held in Halifax, Nova Scotia, between 25 and 28 September, was convened as a result of a proposal from India, and referred to the Executive Committee of the Commonwealth Parliamentary Association by the General Assembly of the Association at its 1984 meeting in the Isle of Man. The Executive Committee endorsed the proposal at its meeting in Cyprus in May 1985.

It was agreed that the Study Group's discussions would be directed to the following subjects: voting rights, electoral systems, electoral procedure, electoral constituencies, candidates, election campaign, election results and judicial review. The objective of the Group, however, was to relate the discussion to the Declaration of Commonwealth Principles (Singapore 1971) wherein the Heads of Government expressed the Commonwealth's commitment to the individual's 'inalienable right to participate by means of free and democratic political processes in framing the society in which they live'.

The first session of the Study Group was convened at 9.30 a.m. on Wednesday, 25 September 1985, in the Red Chamber of Province House, Halifax, with Hon Arthur R. Donahoe, QC, MLA, Speaker of the Nova Scotia House of Assembly, in the Chair.

In his opening remarks, Mr Speaker Donahoe welcomed the delegates on behalf of the Legislature and people of Nova Scotia. He gave a brief account of the history of responsible government in the province, noting that Province House was the site of the first Legislative Assembly and the first responsible government in Canada. While elections were conducted in Nova Scotia prior to 1789, it was in that year that the first Elections Act was enacted and over the intervening years the provincial legislation had been at the forefront of advancements in the electoral field.

Mr Speaker Donahoe advised the Members of the Study Group to acknowledge the financial contribution of the Commonwealth Foundation towards the cost of staging the Study Group meeting in Halifax. At the same time, he suggested that the Group might wish to send a telegram of good wishes to the Deputy Australian Electoral Officer, Mr Andrejs Cirulis, who was prevented from attending the meeting due to illness. The Members of the Study Group agreed unanimously.

Mr Speaker Donahoe then invited nominations for Chairman of the Study Group. Mr Patrick Boyer, MP, the representative from Canada, was unanimously selected.

The Study Group was comprised of Members from seven Branches of the Commonwealth Parliamentary Association, one from each of the seven regions of the Association. The representatives present were:

Chairman: Mr Patrick Boyer, MP (Canada)
Members: Hon C. J. Butale, MP (Botswana)
Shri Somnath Rath, MP (India)
Mr Kenneth L. Shirley, MP (New Zealand)
Hon W. St. Clair-Daniel, CBE, CStJ, JP, MP (Saint Lucia)
Dr Lau Teik Soon, MP (Singapore)
Mr Michael Colvin, MP (United Kingdom)

During their three days of meetings in Halifax, the Study Group Members discussed the various topics on the agenda in light of the principle quoted in the beginning of the preface. In this, they were assisted most competently by their special guests, Mr B. R. Nugent, the Australian Electoral Officer for New South Wales, and Mr Carl Dundas, Special Legal Adviser to the Technical Assistance Group of the Commonwealth Secretariat and a former Electoral Commissioner in Jamaica.

The meetings were also attended by the Chief Electoral Officer of Nova Scotia, Mr D. William MacDonald, and the Chief Election Officer of Ontario, Mr Warren R. Bailie, as well as Mr L. Gofetile, Deputy Clerk of the National Assembly of Botswana. Mr Colin Shepherd, MP, from the United

Kingdom attended a number of sessions and made several valuable contributions to the discussions.

Mr Robert Quayle, Clerk of Tynwald in the Isle of Man, represented the Secretariat of the Commonwealth Parliamentary Association. I, the Chief Electoral Officer of Canada, acted as Rapporteur. In this task, I was very ably assisted by two members of my staff, Ms Christine Jackson and Miss Loren Wells. The staff of the Nova Scotia House of Assembly was also of great assistance.

The Study Group Members generously shared their views on the various subjects which were considered. Their diverse opinions, a reflection of the electoral systems of their own countries, generated a stimulating discussion of all of the items on the agenda.

This Report does not attempt to be a verbatim account of the discussions: rather, it represents a summary of both the presentation of papers and their subsequent discussion, as well as the decisions and resolutions which may have arisen during this four-day period. Study Group Members are not identified individually in their remarks, neither are the guests nor the other participants.

It is my hope that this Report will prove to be of value to all Members of the Commonwealth Parliamentary Association in their future deliberations on electoral law and procedure.

Jean-Marc Hamel

Chairman's Foreword

Wherever Parliamentarians from the Commonwealth gather, and whatever the topic of discussion, the results are inevitably surprising. No matter how well we think we may know the other countries with whom we share the unique Commonwealth bond, every meeting is a fresh voyage of discovery.

At Halifax during the last week of September 1985, Members from each of the seven Commonwealth Parliamentary Association regions gathered, forming a Study Group on election procedures, and once again we proved that for the peaceful evolution of our societies and institutions, nothing exceeds these opportunities for free exchange of ideas. Each of the participating Commonwealth countries had much to contribute, each had something to learn from the others.

The pages of this Report convey to you the essence of our discussions. Anyone who has participated in a conference or study group working session knows all too well how difficult it is to capture, as words on paper, the dynamic interaction of the participants. Thanks to the excellent work of our

Rapporteur, Canada's Chief Electoral Officer, Jean-Marc Hamel, his assistants Loren Wells and Christine Jackson, the Hansard staff of the Nova Scotia House of Assembly, Patsy Gallant, of the Office of the Clerk of the House of Assembly and Mr Speaker Arthur Donahoe's secretary, Nancy Kinsman, all of whom worked extra hard to prepare this report on a short deadline, our ideas are well reflected on the pages which follow.

Yet this Report, no matter how well prepared, cannot really show you the dynamic and positive spirit which pervaded our discussions and indeed our social moments together. This is but to say what we have all long known: the Commonwealth dream becomes a reality when men and women from our many different countries, with our rich diversity of cultures and backgrounds, meet for friendly but frank discussions. Whether as individuals or as countries, we do it better than anyone else because it is 'all in the family'.

Our particular topic, for this Study Group, is electoral procedure and election laws. Too often, in too many of our Commonwealth countries, we take our election laws for granted. Yet, these are a most fundamental body of laws. After all, they are nothing less than the rules we have agreed to follow in order to decide who will acquire political power, and who will lose political power, in our countries. They make the power struggle predictable, and civilized.

As someone with an abiding interest in election law, as evidenced by the fact I have written a number of books on this subject and am currently Chairman of the government caucus policy committee on redistribution and election law in Canada, I was deeply honoured to be elected by the Study Group as Chairman, and delighted with the invaluable exchange of ideas as to how we can all improve the procedures which guarantee free and fair elections in our respective countries.

Each Commonwealth country began with the blueprint of the Westminster parliamentary model, but we have departed from it in many respects, accommodating local political requirements and institutional needs. Although the variations are many, we are all still working with the same core concept: a democracy requires free and open expression of the people's will. The collective wisdom of the people should be heeded, and means must always be found to ensure that it is adequately brought to bear in the governing of our societies.

Our Study Group met at historic Province House in Halifax, and held our meetings in the Red Chamber. Until 1928 the Red Chamber housed the appointed Upper House, or Legislative Council, of the Province of Nova Scotia. It was abolished in that year, as other appointed Upper Houses have been abolished so that all provinces in Canada now are unicameral. This abolition of non-elected legislative bodies in a parliamentary democracy reflects the evolutionary approach which has, over the course of 50 or 100 or 150 years in any of our societies, seen dramatic changes. While none of the changes discussed in this Report are of themselves overly dramatic, their cumulative effect, when adapted as required in particular countries, will continue this important evolution which ensures that our democratic institutions remain true to the central idea – that the voice of the people must be heard and heeded.

J. Patrick Boyer, MP

Introduction

> At their very best, elections are clumsy instruments of choice. In devising the rules for their conduct politicians have wobbled between a pragmatic acceptance of their necessary imperfections and a dream of pure fairness, of achieving a complete match between input – the voters' preferences – and output – the resultant Legislature.

David Butler,
(*Democracy at the Polls*, page 7.
Editors: Butler, Penniman and Ranney. 1981,
American Enterprise Institute for Public Policy
Research, Washington and London.)

It is a generally accepted principle that the democratic process of elections, and indeed any of its various elements, can be fully understood only if examined in the context of the political system in which it operates. The membership of the Study Group – one representative from each of the seven regions of the Commonwealth Parliamentary Association – provided the appropriate setting for a stimulating and informative discussion of the seven topics assigned to the Study Group.

A background paper on each of the seven elements of the democratic electoral process, which had been assigned as topics of discussion for the Study Group, was distributed in advance of the Halifax meeting. These papers, as well as the formal and informal discussions which they provoked, confirmed once again that the democratic electoral process is very dynamic. Although systems and procedures cannot be adopted without some adaptation to the political, cultural or geographical context in which they are to operate, they can contribute effectively to the achievement of the inalienable right of individuals to participate in their society, as espoused in the Declaration of Commonwealth Principles.

The seven topics of discussions were debated in the following order:

1. Electoral Systems
2. Electoral Constituencies
3. Electoral Procedure
4. Voting Rights
5. Candidates
6. Election Campaign
7. Election Results

The order was established with a view to permitting an orderly and chronological examination of the framework within which electors and candidates participate in the democratic process. The discussion of each topic was preceded by a brief introduction by the Chairman and a summary of the relevant paper by its author. Where feasible, an attempt was made following the discussion to identify areas of consensus and to reach a conclusion.

Electoral Systems

Introduction

As David Butler has said in *Democracy at the Polls*, 'an electoral system is a means of translating the popular will into an elected Assembly'. This type of process is usually carried out by means of direct voting on the part of the people. Since they are generally the means through which the will of the people is expressed, most attention has been paid to ways of electing the lower or larger legislative bodies.

The nature of the electoral system adopted by democratic countries varies tremendously from a simple 'first-past-the-post' (FPTP) system, based on single-Member constituencies, to a purely proportional one with a national list of candidates. There are numerous variants within the two extremes, each with its own advantages and disadvantages.

The FPTP system has a number of characteristics: the Member has an attachment to a specific body of constituents; it fosters strong parties and discourages weak ones; decisions are clear-cut and parties must be broad-based; two parties usually predominate and the one with the plurality usually forms the government. However, it may also elect governing parties with the largest number of seats but not necessarily the most votes, as well as so-called minority governments (when the winning party does not have a clear majority of seats).

The other extreme is a purely proportional system, whereby the country is treated as one constituency and the voters choose between any parties that put forward a slate of candidates, and seats in the legislature are allocated in exact proportion to the number of votes obtained. Although fair in the extreme, instability may result due to a proliferation of parties which may lead to insecure coalition governments.

Between the two extremes are a number of variations. Key factors in assessing proportional systems include the constituency size (number of seats per constituency – and therefore the proportion of votes necessary for a party to achieve representation) and the type of formula used for awarding seats based on votes obtained.

As Butler points out, discussion of electoral systems hinges on two conflicting principles: *fairness* and *practicality*. Almost all democracies outside the English-speaking world have moved towards proportional representation (PR). However, most have adapted the pure PR system in the recognition that too many parties make for bad government. As an alternative to, or as an adjunct to, direct voting by the people, some countries for specific reasons (perhaps a large body of uninformed voters) adopt other methods. The appointment of Members to Legislatures usually occurs in connection with Upper Houses, although it can happen in Lower Houses under special circumstances, as is the case in India. Similarly, electoral colleges are often used for constituting Upper Houses (as in France, India), or for electing heads of state (as in the USA and India), an electoral college being a body of electors elected by the people for the purpose of, in turn, electing another body or person or persons. The system is referred to as indirect voting.

Abstract

Paper presented by Shri Somnath Rath, MP, India This discussion paper considers the mechanisms that may be used to 'translate the votes into seats'.

The author classifies electoral systems into three broad categories, namely majority, semi-proportional and proportional systems. A number of forms of each one are outlined and an appraisal given as to their effectiveness. Additional topics discussed include the appointment of Members to Legislatures, the role of electoral colleges and the specific case of the NCMP (non-constituency MP) experience in 1984 in Singapore.

Under the heading of majority systems, the author describes the principal characteristics of the relative majority or plurality system, the block vote, multi-ballot and alternative vote system. He concludes that none results in a legislative body which represents all shades of opinion, although the often artificial majorities gained do tend to lead to strong government.

In the category of semi-proportional systems, the limited vote, single non-transferable and cumulative vote systems and the points system are considered. Generally modified forms of the majority systems, they are used only in multi-Member constituencies and tend to better represent the various opinions of the electors. Their use obliges political parties to select candidates with care so as not to unnecessarily split the vote and results in fairer representation of minor parties. The author concludes that they are not common due to their complex nature and their effect on parties and voters alike.

The proportional representation (PR) category includes discussion of the Hare (or single transferable vote) system and of list systems. The author present the arguments of PR advocates and of its opponents; namely, in the former case, that PR more accurately reflects public opinion and satisfies the minor parties who achieve some level of representation and, in the latter case, that PR breeds instability and coalition governments which ultimately mean the failure of the parliamentary system of government, and that list systems encourage corruption amongst candidates.

The author concludes that appointing Members to Legislatures may have the advantage of ensuring that all sections of society are represented in the Legislature and he also points out the advantages and disadvantages of indirect voting through electoral colleges. The NCMP scheme in Singapore represented a change in Singapore's electoral system designed to guarantee an opposition presence in future Parliaments.

The author concludes that each electoral system is determined in part by the country's geographical situation and historical experience. He quotes Vernon Bogdanor in stating that we must look for a system whose virtues in the context of a particular time and place outweigh its defects.

Discussion

Shri Rath introduced his background paper without attempting to summarize it, in view of its length and complexity. He raised several points which served to focus much of the ensuing discussion. One of these points was a statement that a 'representative body (should be) a true mirror of the opinions of all the eligible people with different interests, ideas about government and approaches to the problems which are faced by the state'. Another was that the purpose of the meeting should be to make an inventory of the systems considered in the discussion paper and to reach conclusions for the consideration of the CPA on how democracy can best be served in the Commonwealth.

An interesting discussion took place, as a result of the aforementioned statement by Shri Rath, respecting the role of the MP. It was suggested that, if MPs were bound by the opinions of their electorates, then the MPs become delegates of the people rather than their representatives. It was also contended that MPs are elected to exercise judgement. The question of conscience votes on moral issues was raised as being one way of releasing MPs from the need to always respect the opinions of their constituents.

The question of the role of an opposition and whether parliamentary democracy could work in a one-party state was discussed at some length. While there was recognition that democracy could indeed exist in a system of 'benign dictatorship' (one-party state), there was general agreement that having at least one opposition party was healthy and necessary. Several means of ensuring political opposition in legislatures were suggested:

1. A constitutional provision for the appointment of Members from parties which have not won representation by election;
2. The creation of an Upper House of appointed Members (UK);
3. The designation of 'opposition Members' within the governing party's own ranks (formerly done in Prince Edward Island in Canada).

On the subject of Upper Houses, it was concluded that the society determines the need. For example, where there is a high degree of literacy amongst Members of the elected body, the need for an Upper House does not arise. Similarly, it may be so difficult to find suitable candidates for the elected Assembly that an Upper House would not be practical.

Also on the subject of oppositions, the point was raised that any system must be able to respond to short-term dislocations, such as the situation which arose in Jamaica in 1983, when the main opposition party boycotted the general election.

In answer to the question as to whether the Commonwealth's basic system of parliamentary democracy, based as it was on the first-past-the-post system, was really 'doing the job', there was general agreement that it was, with the caveat that we were nevertheless always looking for improvements, and the observation that proportional representation had not caused problematic proliferation or fragmentation of parties in Australia (Tasmania and Australian Senate).

In conclusion, the Study Group decided that the basic principles of parliamentary democracy were still acceptable in the Commonwealth, although each country had adapted them to meet its own circumstances and societal needs, and was constantly looking for improvements. In fact, it was suggested that the population's fundamental freedom to express its preference and elect the representatives of its choice should be more important than the system used to translate votes into seats/representation.

Electoral Constituencies

Introduction

The establishment of constituency boundaries is one of the most fundamental elements of the electoral system in a parliamentary democracy. It is essential to ensure fairness. The determination of the boundaries must take into account whether the electoral system is a majority system, a semi-proportional or proportional type of system. There is also variation in the number of Members each constituency will return. Thus, there are single or multi-Member constituencies.

Since the establishment of the electoral boundaries may directly affect the outcome of the election, the process must be perceived by the electorate as having been devised, and must be devised, in an atmosphere which is as impartial as possible, while still recognizing the diverse interests inherent in a particular region or community.

In a number of democracies, the responsibility for the setting of electoral boundaries, as well as the frequency of this undertaking, are prescribed by law, so as to keep the process as free from public controversy as possible. This task may be performed following a general census or a general election. There may also be a requirement that the procedures be standardized and the decisions of those to whom the task is assigned open to public scrutiny. Indeed, in many cases, provisions are made for the public to make representations in this regard.

There are many factors which must be taken into consideration in determining constituency boundaries, a major one being equality among the constituents. While strict adherence to the principle of 'one man – one vote' may not be possible to achieve, the factors that will dictate the extent of the tolerance from the quotient should be clearly spelled out. Community of interest, community of identity, or historical patterns in an area are but a few factors that have to be considered. In some countries it may also be necessary to take into account the geographical size of the constituencies in sparsely populated areas in order to keep them manageable. Whether the boundaries should be established on the basis of the total population or only the adult population is also a question to be answered.

However, population statistics are only one criterion because they provide merely a mathematical perspective of the situation. Other criteria which must be considered are ease of communication and transportation, as well as the topographical features of the country or its regions. These factors may influence the ability of an elected representative to adequately represent his constituents; as well they may affect the ease of access by the electorate to polling facilities.

There are thus a number of conflicting factors to be reconciled. Under the principle of 'representation by population', constituencies should be as numerically equal as possible. It may, however, become very difficult for an elected representative to adequately articulate the diverse interests which may have to be included in one electoral district. Therefore, a decision may have to be made whether to apply strict statistical rules or to consider other factors and allow for their inclusion into this basic part of the electoral system – the setting of constituency boundaries.

Abstract

Paper presented by Mr Kenneth L. Shirley, MP, New Zealand The system by which a democracy defines the boundaries of its electoral constituencies is of fundamental importance particularly for countries where Parliamentarians are elected on a 'first-past-the-post' basis. The placement of constituency boundaries could have an impact on the electoral fortunes of a particular party or candidate. In consideration of this, in New Zealand the revision of the boundaries was removed from the parliamentary arena and made the responsibility of a special statutory body, known as the Representation Commission.

The membership of the commission is carefully balanced to ensure impartiality and the fairest redistribution possible. Four of the eight members are non-political public servants, one member is a government appointee, two are political appointees and the Chairman is traditionally a District Court judge.

Redistribution is undertaken in New Zealand every five years following the quinquennial census when the electoral boundaries for the general electorate are redrawn, as are those of the four Maori seats provided by legislation. The Electoral Act sets out the basic requirements, considerations and rules that the commission is to follow. The commission, however, is free to set its own procedures.

Once the necessary quota has been established, the commission must also consider several factors: the existing boundaries of electoral districts, community of interest, facilities of communication and topographical features. Only a variation of five per cent is allowed from the established quota in order to ensure that each MP will represent the same number of constituents. A low tolerance reduces the threat of gerrymandering. Provisions exists to allow the public to have an input in the commission's recommendations.

The legislative provisions were designed to strictly adhere to the principle of 'one vote – one value' and because of statutory entrenchment, redistribution in New Zealand is an automatic process that is as far removed from political interference as possible.

Recently, a Royal Commission was appointed to examine the electoral system. Contentious matters that are likely to receive attention are: whether electoral boundaries should be drawn less frequently than every five years, whether a five per cent tolerance is still acceptable, and whether or not total population or adult population should be considered when establishing the boundaries.

Discussion

Following the presentation of Mr Shirley's paper, the Chairman took a few moments to summarize some of the major points which he felt were of particular interest to the Study Group and could perhaps be useful in initiating the discussion.

In his remarks, he raised the issue of the tolerance, that is, how far the population of a constituency could deviate from the quota established for a state or a province. The intervals between the readjustments of boundaries, and whether total population or adult population should be the basis for establishing constituencies, were other issues that he raised. In addition, it was felt that the Group could perhaps focus on several other issues, such as: whether this task should be completely removed from the Parliamentarians and assigned to an independent body; who would comprise such a body; whether the political parties should be permitted to make submissions or representations to this body: the recognition of minority groups in the setting of constituency boundaries, and finally, what mechanisms could or should be provided to allow for drastic shifts in population, especially where this might result in the loss of representation for a particular area.

It was indicated that removing the responsibility for setting the boundaries from the hands of the politicians generally had a very positive effect and was well accepted by the public.

Some concern was expressed over frequent redistribution, as this might have a negative effect on the Member and his electorate. It might be difficult for an elected Member, subjected to frequent change, to develop any type of identity with his constituents and it might present difficulties in this respect for the electors as well. Political parties might not be given time for reorganization if short intervals between redistributions were the case, nor might they be allowed sufficient opportunity to make submissions to the commissions. Automatic triggering of redistribution provided in law, but with longer time spans in between, might be the ideal. There should, however, be some provisions that will place an obligation on the government to carry this through as there might be occasions when implementation is deliberately delayed. The government should have no discretion in the matter.

Another suggestion made was to allow for some commonality in the boundaries at the various levels of governments. While this might make meeting the quota within an acceptable tolerance more difficult, it could be a useful guideline to ensure continuity in boundaries.

The Group also reviewed some of the various forms of appointing commissioners or other persons responsible for the delimitation of constituencies. There was considerable variation in this connection. The commissioners might include the Speaker, judges, the Surveyor-General, representatives of the Post Office, et cetera.

The Study Group then went on to the question of a possible interim review of the boundaries. It was explained that there were jurisdictions which had special committees, mathematical formulae or a petitioning process to indicate that change might be necessary, either on a country-wide basis or in a particular area only.

The officials charged with the delimitation of the boundaries were at times accused of being concerned only with numbers and of ignoring other factors, such as community of interest, community of identity or historical patterns. Since a realistic tolerance level might be difficult to establish, these other factors might have to be given more emphasis.

One must also consider possible repercussions if areas were to lose seats through population shifts. There might then be a need for recognized safeguards in order to protect against this possibility.

The discussion then moved on to the concept of limiting the constant growth in the number of elected Members. This was of particular relevance in jurisdictions which were experiencing pressure to increase representation even if the legislative Chamber could not accommodate the increase. The Group Members were of the opinion that importance should be given to the sense of intimacy or collegiality which needed to be felt in such a body; yet it was also recognized that legislators might have difficulty reconciling this with the need for adequate representation of the population.

In conclusion, the Group Members expressed the view that in redistributing electoral boundaries, equality of representation should be one of the main guiding principles. The principle of 'one vote – one value' should be uppermost, while not precluding consideration of the political, legal and institutional factors.

Electoral Procedure

Introduction

As David Butler has pointed out in *Democracy at the Polls*, 'the right to vote is not enough: the administrative procedures must be adequate for its exercise'.

Election administrators Since procedures can only be administered by people, it is essential that the people who are appointed must be seen to be trustworthy and impartial in their actions. The method of choosing the Chief Electoral Officer or commission is therefore of key importance.

The election period The length of election campaigns can vary from less than four weeks to more than two years, depending on such factors as whether the legislature in question has a fixed term (as in the case of the USA) and whether the method of voter registration requires the compilation of new electoral lists after the calling of the election (as in Canada).

Aside from the administrative requirements of the electoral system, other factors must also be considered in determining the length and dates of campaigns. These include the advantages of a short period for the party in power over opposition parties, the effect of a long campaign on the interest and participation of the electorate, and the time period prescribed for purposes of determining the election expenses of parties and candidates.

Registration of electors and electoral lists Any democratic electoral system designed to put the 'one man – one vote' principle into practice must first provide that, to the greatest possible degree, only those people who are qualified to vote actually do so, and secondly, that people do not vote on more than one occasion. The most common method is to prepare a list of all qualified electors based on the nature of the frachise as laid down in the relevant legislation. Its forms include permanent lists, continuous rolls, annual enumerations or enumerations conducted after the calling of an election.

At the heart of determining the registration method to be used lies a philosophical issue: should the onus for registration rest with the state or with the individual. Once this is decided, there remains the question of open or closed lists, and, if the latter, when they should be closed. New human rights legislation (such as the Canadian Charter of Rights and Freedoms) may have a profound effect on the limitations on registration which are currently imposed in many jurisdictions.

Computerization of electoral lists, the consequences of privacy legislation and the use of electoral lists for reasons other than elections are all contemporary issues.

The relationship between the type of registration system chosen and the participation of electors is frequently studied but it is difficult to reach conclusions. Compulsory registration is an interesting proposition but, for some, it has unpleasant overtones, especially in societies becoming increasingly dehumanized by modern technology.

Ballot papers and voting machines A standard format for ballot papers ensures that: a) fake marked ballots do not find their way into ballot boxes for counting, and b) the chances of spoiled and rejected ballots are minimized.

Voting machines can be used to speed up counting votes, lessen the chances of human error in calculating results, make possible the calculation of sub-totals at periodic intervals during election day, and reduce manpower requirements. Their value, however, is considered highly questionable in systems that require the elector to vote for only one candidate in a simple plurality system.

Absentee voting In any democracy operating on a basis that the exercise of the franchise should be facilitated as much as possible, mechanisms for voting by absent electors must be considered. Key considerations relate to the residence requirements of electors and the implications on government of results delayed by ballots not received in time for counting on election day.

Once categories of eligible electors have been determined, possible coping mechanisms include proxy voting, the postal vote and use of a write-in ballot (for example, the Canadian armed forces voting system). In the case of electors residing abroad, the latter two mechanisms require the institution of permanent lists and self-registration and de-registration by electors. All systems of absentee voting are subject to greater than usual chances of abuse.

Compulsory voting Most legal codes reflect a belief in the democratic theory that the people form a sovereign body comprising individuals who share equally in the right to vote and have the choice of exercising that right or not. The rationale for compulsory voting is always that it is better to vote than not to vote.

The effect of the compulsion on turnout is difficult to determine, since so many other factors can influence turnout.

Policing the system Procedures to ensure fair and free elections necessitate mechanisms for the prevention or minimization of abuse. Provision must therefore be made for defining election offences, illegal acts and corrupt practices, the penalties for commission of same, and means of enforcing those provisions. In addition, careful consideration should be given to the question of who should be responsible for conducting inquiries and investigations and for instituting prosecutions.

Abstract

Paper presented by Mr Michael Colvin, MP, United Kingdom Mr Colvin's discussion paper considers several aspects of electoral procedure within the context of the British system and experience, such as: electoral commissions and officers, the minimum election period, the registration of voters and compilation of the electoral roll, absentee voting and compulsory voting. Additional background material is provided on recent proposals for electoral change in Britain by way of summaries of the House of Commons Home Affairs Committee Report, 1982/3, and the government reply of January 1984, together with a paper on the electoral registration system in Britain and a paper on aspects of compulsory voting.

The author stresses that all electoral law and procedure is designed to put into practice the principle of free and fair elections. In this regard, the role of election officials is fundamental; these individuals must be well established and respected in the local community, preferably occupying some other post of public trust between elections. In Britain the well-established local government system meets these needs.

The minimum election period varies among countries according to law, custom and the administrative demands of whatever election system is in place. Doubt is expressed as to the existence of an optimum length of campaign and considerations of voter apathy and political organization time are raised.

In dealing with the question of voter registration and electoral rolls, the author starts with the basic premise that electoral lists should be as accurate as possible in terms of the qualifications of those on the list, but that a balance should be struck to guard against possible abuse. In Britain, the level of inaccuracy of the electoral lists is a concern which raises the spectre of compulsory registration. However, this raises serious questions relating to enforcement and infringement on personal liberty. Consideration is given to the idea of continuous updating of lists and to reasonable dates for closing lists.

Absentee voting is discussed in the context of facilitating the franchise while guarding against abuse. The author distinguishes between the different categories of absent electors and the alternative mechanisms which are available. In each case he enunciates the problems encountered in accommodating them in Britain. As for compulsory voting, the issues are raised but are not resolved. Primary among them are considerations of personal liberty and the effect of compulsion on voter participation.

Discussion

Mr Colvin introduced the subject by observing that the 'one vote – one value' concept would not be possible if the 'nuts and bolts' of the system – the detailed procedures – were not in place. It is in this area, he observed, that the greatest differences existed between the countries of the Commonwealth. As an illustration of the view that each Commonwealth country was constantly looking towards improving, he pointed out that the UK's Representation of the People Act had been amended nine times in the last ten years.

Before introducing his paper, Mr Colvin posed the question as to how each country could best establish mechanisms for the review of its electoral procedures. He suggested that such a review could be corrected either on an on-going basis by, for example, a permanent select (or standing) parliamentary committee, as is the case in the UK and Canada, or on an *ad hoc* basis by a specially constituted committee with a specific mandate to review the relevant legislation.

The UK Member then outlined some of the specific features of the British electoral procedures described in his paper. In addition, he raised the question of how to ensure that there was fair play during elections. He concluded with a quotation from Edmund Burke which he felt was particularly appropriate: 'A state without the means of some change is without the means of its conservation.'

Due to the comprehensive nature of the subject and the limited time available for its review, the Study Group's discussions focused on the aspects of compulsory and multiple voting, compulsory and multiple registration, the length of election periods and the role of international observers.

The subject of compulsory voting stimulated a particularly lively discussion with two jurisdictions, Singapore and Australia, explaining the basic principles behind compulsory voting in their respective countries. In the case of Singapore, it was introduced in 1959 to counteract the poor electoral participation of the majority ethnic group in the population (Chinese) during the colonial period. In Australia, it was introduced in 1924 for federal elections, when Parliamentarians began to be concerned over the drop in percentage turnout at elections from the 90s at the turn of the century to the low 70s by 1922.

While most Group Members did not express support for compulsory voting, probably because of the notion of coercion, the representatives of Singapore and Australia felt that it was more a question of duty than of coercion which resulted in electors feeling a sense of responsibility for and interest in the governments they elected.

One observation about the effect of compulsory voting was that it meant that the parties had more time and energy to spend on the substance of their political campaigns rather than on mobilizing the electorate through large numbers of campaign workers.

Multiple registration of electors would seem to be a problem only in those jurisdictions which did not have computerized electoral lists because multiple entries could be screened out and deleted from the master computerized list.

As for the problem of multiple voting, some countries, such as those in the Caribbean, stained the fingers of electors with a substance which was visible only under ultra-violet light, thereby making it impossible for an elector to vote more than once, while other computerized jurisdictions were able to screen out and prosecute electors who had voted more than once.

No conclusion was reached on the question on the length of election periods. While most jurisdictions had legislated at least the maximum and/or minimum periods, the actual length of the period hinged on the time required to complete certain electoral necessities, such as the enumeration of electors (Canada), the revision of voters' lists (Australia) or the printing and distribution of ballot papers. Opinions differ greatly on this issue depending on whether one is an election administrator or a politician!

Some consideration was given to the role of international election observers and a book entitled *Guidelines for International Election Observing* (1984) was brought to the Group's attention. It was prepared by Larry Garber for the International Human Rights Law Group, an American organization established in 1978. One participant felt that such observers were only valuable when there was evidence of social and political disturbance in a country, because the sovereignty of each state must be fully respected, while another repeated a suggestion that a permanent Commonwealth team of election observers might be trained for mobilization as and when needed.

Voting Rights

Introduction

An important principle of democracy is that as many of the citizens as possible in a society should be permitted to participate in the choice of those who will represent and govern them. The people must be allowed the opportunity to enjoy this privilege with as few restrictions as possible. The results of their participation determine who shall be entrusted with their political well-being.

Voting rights have evolved considerably over the years as a result of pressures of different types. Often, the society will dictate to the legislators the extent of the franchise. At times, influences will intervene. For instance the First World War was instrumental in bringing about female suffrage in Canada, while women had to wait until after the Second World War to be enfranchised in France.

The granting of the franchise is also influenced by certain qualifications that are required in order that the elector will use his vote wisely and responsibly. These qualifications will invariably differ from country to country, not only in their nature, but in the degree to which they are applied. They are usually the product of the experience of the particular country in question, of traditions, cultural environment, et cetera. The qualifications may relate to age, property ownership, sex, residency, citizenship, degree of literacy, or language.

In order to protect the integrity of the franchise, restrictions may be imposed. Although the tendency would seem to point in the direction of as few restrictions as possible, some individuals are still disqualified from the exercise of the franchise. The reasons for disqualification may include mental incompetency, a criminal record, being found guilty of a corrupt practice related to an election, or the holding of special status, such as that of a judge or tribal chief.

Once the rules for the granting of the right to vote have been established, they should be entrenched in the law so that this right will be protected. After all, it is one of the most fundamental in a democracy.

Abstract

Paper presented by Hon W. St Clair-Daniel, CBE, CStJ, JP, MP, Saint Lucia One of the principles fundamental to parliamentary democracy developed centuries ago by Aristotle is that government should rest upon the consent of the many, who should have the opportunity to express their consent. One of the ways in which this consent may be regularly expressed is during elections. In order to show that it truly recognizes the consent of the citizens, a parliamentary government must clearly indicate that recognition through legislative enactments and opportunity. If this consent is truly to exist, the government must allow as wide as possible a base to permit this. The debate has continued over the years as to just how broad this base should be. In parliamentary democracies, there is now universal acceptance that substantially all citizens should have a right to be heard in the selection of their governments, although the conditions placed upon the exercise of this right may vary.

Various factors are taken into consideration in granting the franchise. One of the most crucial ones is age. Generally, it has been related to that of legal majority, although in today's society there is great demand to lower the voting age. Perhaps the ideal criterion should not be age but the ability to use this privilege with responsibility. Other factors which should be considered when dealing with a community and its political authority are citizenship and residency. In addition, sex, literacy and language qualifications at times play a role, although they alone must not be invoked to eliminate any from the franchise. Once the qualifications for enfranchisement have been established, limitations may be introduced on the basis of mental competency, criminal behaviour or by reason of the holding of some special status or position within the community.

Discussion

In beginning his presentation, Mr St Clair-Daniel indicated in his preamble that his paper was not to be considered an overall view of voting rights in the Caribbean. The supplementary paper distributed to delegates would provide them with that background information. He would attempt, he said, to look at the different aspects of voting rights – the age of majority, the citizenship and residency requirements, sex, literacy, language, qualifications, grounds for disqualification, and the special positions of certain groups of individuals.

Several of the Group Members raised the issue of what measures should be taken, if any, to allow voting by eligible voters who were out of the country at election time. In a number of the jurisdictions represented by Members of the Study Group, much debate was arising at present with respect to members of the armed services, public servants abroad, in addition to those who were absent on business. One Member expressed the opinion that these people had the same right to vote as those who were in the country, since the election results would have a direct bearing on their lives as well, and mechanisms should therefore be instituted in order that they might cast a ballot.

There might be complications inherent in this type of extension of the vote, such as whether a spouse should be allowed to select his/her own constituency and whether the eligibility of those voting under these provisions should only be in effect for an absence of a specific length, together with an indication that the voter intended to return. In effect, a long absence could be construed as an intention of staving permanently away.

Once the eligibility of those individuals had been decided, mechanisms and procedures must be put in place to ensure that their ballots would be cast and counted. This might require some unusual means such as radio transmission and special couriers, but in every case the secrecy of the ballot must be preserved.

Special innovations such as proxy voting and mail-in ballots might assist voters who, although not absent from their country of residence, might be absent from their own constituency at voting time. In addition, mobile polls might be used to assist disabled electors and those in hospitals and institutions. The delegates concluded that while innovative methods might be developed to ensure that the ballots of as many eligible people as possible might be cast, individual states must ensure that these were accompanied by appropriate safeguards to protect the process from abuse and fraud.

The participants also discussed briefly the limitations with respect to age, change of residence, and rights of prisoners to vote in the various countries they represented.

The question was raised as to what forms of redress were available to persons who, through administrative error and no fault of their own, had been disfranchised. One comment in reply was that in some jurisdictions, the onus was on the electors to determine if their names were on the list and if not, to take the necessary steps to correct the situation.

The so-called 'silent list' in place in Australia and New Zealand was described. It was a system designed to protect certain individuals from harassment or violence.

Illiteracy was recognized as a potential barrier that might be used to deny people the franchise. The Members of the Study Group examined suggestions regarding the ways in which the varying degrees of literacy found in the Commonwealth might be accommodated in electoral systems, both in an administrative and political way. In their exchange, they explained the practices used in their own countries, which included the use of photographic placards, symbols on the ballots, education programmes and audio-visual aids

It was emphasized that there were two aspects to this problem. On the one hand, election administrators must be able to explain to illiterate electors what their duties were in the electoral process, while on the other, the candidates themselves must be able to communicate with those electors. The Study Group concluded that with regard to election administration, any technique which would facilitate the removal of the barrier of illiteracy from the electoral process should be encouraged.

In establishing polling places, the Study Group emphasized several points that they felt would contribute to a more desirable situation. Election administrators should be asked to find locations which were politically neutral, as opposed to private residences of those associated with a particular political interest. The places chosen should also be as accessible as possible to the electors. This did not only mean in their location, but also referred to level access for entering the premises. Another suggestion was that an inventory of polling places should be maintained to facilitate the establishment of these locations in advance and retain continuity in the locations used.

The final segment of the discussion on voting rights centred on the verification of the identity of persons as eligible electors. The Group Members recognized that this was not only a problem in developing countries where there were large population shifts, but in other countries as well where people were becoming more transient. New provisions might have to be introduced into legislation to recognize this factor. Some countries already used identity cards or required declarations at the polling place.

Candidates

Introduction

According to Professor Terence Qualter in his book *The Election Process in Canada* (McGraw-Hill, 1970):

> A completely open election would, presumably, be one in which anybody could vote for anybody. But, outside some very small groups and associations, such free-wheeling procedure is not a serious possibility. The choice of electors must, for all practical purposes, be confined to some more or less formally recognized 'slate' of candidates.

He goes on to say:

> If the mass of electors are reduced to choosing from among a set of candidates pre-selected by a small unrepresentative elite, then the democracy is a fake and its electoral institutions a mere facade. Again, if the social and economic pressures of candidacy and membership are such as to discourage or bar all but the chosen few, then the reality of democracy is restrained and inhibited.
>
> On the other hand, if there were no winnowing process, if there were to be hundreds of thousands of candidates for every elective position, then representative government would likely collapse in anarchy.

In this context. Professor Qualter suggests that the question of candidacy can be usefully considered under three headings, namely, the *legal*, the *political*, and the *socio-economic*.

The *legal* considerations include the qualifications that are required to be eligible as a candidate and the procedures which must be followed to make candidacy official. The *political* considerations include both the processes by which the parties select their candidates and the extent to which the customary political practices make formal endorsement by a recognized party a virtual necessity. The *socio-economic* considerations include those factors which will determine the chances of being selected as a candidate and then being elected. They are inseparably linked to the political.

Legal qualifications of candidates Most commonly the qualification for candidacy is that the person must be qualified as an elector. Residency in the constituency where the candidate is running is not normally required. However, the age discrepancy between the qualifications of electors as opposed to candidates may be questionable.

Disqualifications may centre around offences committed against the election legislation or under the criminal code.

Political affiliation and nomination Elections in multi-party democracies are now basically contests between political parties in which candidates are important to the extent that they are representative of parties.

Generally, a candidate wishing to run under a particular party label must first obtain the approval of his or her fellow party members. Undoubtedly the use of party labels affects a candidate's chances of election. However, the provisions for a candidate to run independently from the parties is important in a free and democratic system.

In almost all cases, whether running under a party label or not, candidates must be able to obtain a certain measure of support from the electors in their constituencies. Also, they must be able to raise sufficient funds to make a financial deposit at the time of official nomination. In this regard, philosophy varies between reducing or abolishing deposits in favour of increasing the level of support required from electors, and increasing the amount of deposit – all in an attempt to 'weed out' the seemingly non-serious candidates who sometimes might appear to be out to make a mockery of the democratic system as we know it. Reimbursement of the deposit of the candidate who wins more than a specified percentage of the votes cast would not seem to be a very effective deterrent to the non-serious candidate, unless the deposit represents a large amount of money.

Socio-economic considerations It goes without saying that, in a democratic society, a person should be able to run as a candidate regardless of their sex, religion, property status, ethnic origin or financial means.

Abstract

Paper presented by Dr Lau Teik Soon, MP, Singapore In considering the selection of candidates for election to the popularly elected (or lower) Chambers, the discussion paper deals with two main factors, namely, the legal requirements of candidacy (in terms of qualifications to be a candidate) and the political considerations of the parties. The first is examined in a general way in the context of some Commonwealth countries, while the second is considered in light of the unique selection procedure of the governing party in Singapore (People's Action Party (PAP)). Appended to the paper are comparative tables on the respective qualifications of electors and candidates in the Commonwealth countries and on the basic requirements for the official nomination of a candidate. Also appended to the paper is a table recording the performance of the PAP in the period from 1959 to 1984.

In terms of the legal requirements for candidacy, the author compares the age, nationality and residence requirements for candidates in several Commonwealth countries to illustrate the point that potential Parliamentarians should be better educated and more knowledgeable about national issues than the average voter in order to effectively represent his or her constituency.

Similar comparisons are made of the major disqualifications of candidates and of the requirements for elector support and financial deposits in the official nomination process.

With respect to the selection of candidates by parties, the author observes that the 'ideal' candidate is probably one who has the right mix of 'grassroots' appeal and professional or technocratic know-how. The specific case of the selection method used by the PAP in Singapore prior to the December 1984 general election is examined to demonstrate that the major issue now facing the PAP is one of succession – whether or not the party can train enough young men and women to take over the leadership of the government during the next fifteen years. He outlines the qualities currently being sought by the PAP in its candidates and profiles the sitting Members in terms of the desired criteria.

Candidates for the PAP in Singapore in 1984 were selected by the Central Executive Committee (CEC). They had to successfully complete a series of informal and formal interviews, including a written test, and submit several character references. Panel interviews conducted by the Prime Minister and cabinet Members followed. Of some 400 original potential candidates, only about 30 were chosen to represent the PAP. These were then required to submit to a psychological assessment and intelligence test.

While recognizing the PAP's selection method might not be suitable for all Commonwealth countries, the author concludes that an increasingly complex technological world demands that its political leaders be the better educated, more capable and more successful members of society. He recommends the approach as a goal for other Commonwealth countries.

Discussion

Following the Chairman's introduction of the subject, Dr Lau briefly summarized the highlights of his paper, including an outline of the process used by the PAP to select its candidates for the 1984 Singapore general election. In making his summary of the various qualifications of candidates, Dr Lau observed that, in comparing the legal requirements for candidacy in the various Commonwealth countries, it was noteworthy that they often differed from the legal requirements to be an elector. For example, the legal age for voting in the UK was 18 years, whereas the age for candidacy was 21 years; in India the respective ages were 21 and 25 years. Similarly, some jurisdictions required a specific length of residency in the country as a prerequisite to candidacy.

It was noted that no comparison of electoral procedures seemed to exist for the Commonwealth countries and it was unanimously agreed that a recommendation should be made to the CPA that a compendium be drafted to include comparative data on the following subjects: electoral systems, constituencies, procedures, voting rights, candidates, campaigns, reporting results and judicial review.

One part of the ensuing discussion centred on the personal qualities required for candidacy. While the PAP in Singapore selected its candidates on the basis of intelligence, honesty and proven ability (following a stringent assessment process by the Central Executive Committee), some Study Group Members expressed the view that candidates must be in touch with the grassroots and that perhaps there were already too many professionals and technocrats in the Legislatures. A more conciliatory observation was that candidates must be able to contribute to the parliamentary process and accept their responsibility to respect the electoral process.

There was also considerable discussion of the role of the central party organizations in the process of selecting candidates. While in Singapore the PAP's local party branches could nominate people to be candidates, the final decision rested with the Central Executive Committee. However, in certain other countries such as the UK and Canada, the central party executive could make suggestions but the final decision rested with the local branch. In the case of Canada, the leader of the party provided written endorsement of the chosen candidate so that, in case of a dispute over candidacy at the local level, the party had to resolve the dispute rather than leave it to the election administrators. Naturally, the selection process used depended on the constitution of the political party in question and was not enshrined in the election law.

The general opinion of Group Members tended towards the view that the selection of candidates should, as far as possible, be the responsibility of local party branches rather than central party committees to promote morale and loyalty within the party.

The incidence of 'frivolous' candidates and parties was discussed at some length in the context of the experience of three jurisdictions – the UK, Australia and Canada. An extreme example was cited: the case of the 1 March 1984 Chesterfield by-election (UK) when a total of seventeen candidates appeared on the ballot, of whom fourteen were 'fringe' party candidates or independents, and only three retained their deposits. Some Group Members felt that there was a place for 'frivolous' party candidates, as a means of 'letting off steam' more or less harmlessly. Indeed, denying status to groups or individuals might, at times, drive them underground. However, it was felt that there ought to be, at the same time, some sort of screening process in order to protect the system.

As for the particular screening process to be used, discussion centred on increasing nomination deposits and/or increasing the number of electors' names a candidate must collect in his/her nomination papers.

The Chairman proposed that the Group recommend to the CPA a re-examination of the legal requirements for nomination in the Commonwealth countries, with a view to establishing what would be an acceptable threshold number of electors' signatures and an amount for the deposit that would be meaningful in today's terms.

Other items raised in the discussion included the effects of introducing election financing on candidacy (as in Canada). It was felt that the reimbursement of election expenses (in turn, controlled by limits established by law) created access to membership in Legislatures which might otherwise be restricted to candidates of some personal means. However, for such a process to work properly, there must be a system in place to register political parties and candidates.

The role of women in the Legislatures was raised briefly and it was recognized that there was a need to increase the numbers of women participating in the parliamentary process.

Election Campaign

Introduction

In any type of political system, it is important to ensure that mechanisms have been put into place which will create, especially during an election campaign, an impartial balance between differing factions. Not only does this include a non-partisan body to administer the electoral process, but it also requires the clarification of corrupt campaigning practices, the safeguarding of the freedom of assembly, and, as in some countries, strict application of rules and regulations controlling the funding of political parties and candidates.

The candidates must be confident that the environment in which they are conducting their campaign is free from any interference. They must be satisfied that their rights, enshrined in legislation that is administered by persons who are perceived as being above political influence, will be protected and that penalties will be imposed for any form of electoral fraud or corrupt practices committed by the participants themselves.

Freedom of assembly is one of the basic freedoms in a democracy. In today's modern world, however, growing emphasis is now being placed on equal access to the various media, particularly the broadcasting media. In increasing numbers, campaigners are finding that this is the most effective way to reach the electorate. In response to this development, individual states are establishing controls over the use of this facility to ensure reasonable access to all candidates and political partics .

It has been argued that the publication of opinion poll results during elections constitutes a form of undue influence on voters and should be prohibited. Others dispute this, saving that the results are factual information which electors are entitled to consider as they please and that, unless polls are fully prohibited, the alternative to publication is the exclusive use of this information by political elites in ways which would not be, as is now the case, open to public scrutiny.

One of the major influences on the conduct of a campaign is, however, the financing of the political parties and candidates. The extent to which disclosure of funding or expenditures is revealed varies from one electoral jurisdiction to another, as does the degree to which the political entities are provided with subsidies from public funds. These subsidies may be provided in an indirect manner, such as by means of tax credits to contributors, or directly, by re-imbursement of a portion of election expenses incurred, annual payments by the state to political parties, or by funding the parliamentary caucus of a political party.

In order to provide for some equality in an election campaign, some jurisdictions limit the amount of election expenses which may be incurred by political parties or candidates and provide for severe sanctions if this limit is not adhered to.

The challenge remains to strike a balance between the need to establish campaign practices which will permit broad participation, while not leaving the system open to abuse.

Abstract

Paper presented by Mr Patrick Boyer, MP, Canada In Canada, the legislation governing the electoral campaign has evolved over many years; but, in recent years, legislative changes have been adopted which serve to bring the system closer to the ideal of equity. Canadians are protected by the constitution from indefinite delays in the calling of elections to serve partisan purposes. They can also be confident that these elections are administered by a totally impartial organization, created in 1920, and headed by the Chief Electoral Officer, who is accountable directly and only to Parliament.

There are now strict legislative provisions which govern the use of broadcast time by political parties and ensure access to the media.

The doctrine of agency, which was recently extended to parties, has become an integral part of the control and disclosure of election expenses and contributions. Parties and candidates are now given direct subsidies through partial re-imbursement of their expenses and indirect financial assistance through tax credits for contributions made to their campaigns. These new rules emphasize open financing of political parties and candidates and encourage small contributions. Grants are also made to the elected Members of Parliament directly or through their caucus. In addition, restrictions have been removed on public opinion polls as the general feeling is that although they are generally accurate, they dc not necessarily influence voters. The right to meet, a cornerstone of democracy, existed in fact long before it was formally guaranteed by law.

A more demanding and less tolerant public is pushing for reform. Electoral reformers must face the challenge of preventing abuse without limiting freedom.

Discussion

The paper on this topic was presented by Mr Patrick Boyer, MP, of Canada and described the election campaign in the Canadian context. In summarizing his paper. Mr Boyer focused mainly on the question of the financing of elections, describing the fundamental principles underlying the Canadian system.

The discussion first centred on the allocation of broadcasting time to the various political organizations. Concern was expressed that all political groups in the system, whether well-established or newly-formed, should be considered on the basis of a formula which was fair to all.

The Chairman then asked for contributions from each of the Group Members on the question of election expenses as this had such an important effect on election campaigns. The provisions varied greatly among the jurisdictions, some limiting contributions, others having ceilings on expenditures. There were also various other facets to this such as free mailings, re-imbursement of election expenses, annual subsidies to political parties or direct grants to a political party's caucus. One main item which was common among the jurisdictions was the concept of disclosure. If any of the legislative provisions were breached, and found by public scrutiny or examination, the sanctions could be quite severe and could even result in the loss of the seat or in a jail term. The doctrine of agency was also paramount in any aspect of this, as an agent was not only accountable for himself alone, but for the candidate as well.

The conclusion reached by the Study Group was that steps should be taken to ensure that the political process was open and accessible to all who wished to be candidates and that the rules were established so that financial means would not decide who might, or might not, participate.

With respect to spending limits, they should be such as to adequately control the situation. They should not be so low as to be unrealistic, nor should they be so high that they do not in effect create any limit at all.

Limits on expenses or similar controls would produce results only if the responsibility to ensure their enforcement was clearly assigned to an individual or body who had realistic powers of investigation.

Disclosure and openness were also of paramount importance.

Lack of political neutrality was raised as a problem found in developing countries, however the consensus arrived at was that this phenomenon occurred in most jurisdictions, although there were ways of dealing with it. Political impartiality and competence were values which had to be balanced in the selection of election administrators. The definition of political impartiality might differ from one territory to another. Unless one could be prepared to accept someone with a political background of some degree, those chosen might have difficulties understanding the electoral process. One solution might be to relieve the local people of as many weighty administrative decisions as possible. These could be decided at the central level by those who had the ongoing responsibility for the election machinery. If the machinery was seen as being impartial, then the whole system should be perceived as fair. Encouragement should be given to young people to consider a career in electoral administration so that they were then beyond political interference.

Election administrators had been given an expanded role in some jurisdictions: conducting the census and the votes of trade unions, evaluating the indemnities paid to elected Members, and the administration of ethical conduct regulations.

Above all, some continuity in the individuals involved should be maintained for this was reflected then in their independent status. They might otherwise be seen as susceptible or vulnerable to partisan influence and the public would, therefore, lose confidence in their decisions.

In discussing the holding of by-elections, the Study Group resolved that these should be called without undue delay when a constituency had lost its Member, subject to a reasonable limit of perhaps no more than six months. This would accommodate the possibility of a by-election being required towards the end of a Parliament or during a time when climatic conditions were not particularly favourable.

The impact of opinion polls during an election was examined While 'success loves success' and polls might influence some voters to support those who appeared to be leading, this was usually counter-balanced by those who tended to side with the underdog. The consensus, however, was that measures should be taken to ensure that polls would be honest. Consequently, the Study Group ended this session with a recommendation that while public opinion polls should not be prohibited, they should be subject to a kind of consumer protection legislation. The public had a right to know who commissioned the poll, at what cost, when it was taken, how large a sample was used, what the normal margin of error was, and other questions of this nature.

Election Results

Introduction

For elections to be fair and honest, it is not enough that the law provides for votes to be cast freely and secretly, without coercion of any sort on the voters or undue restrictions or constraints on the candidates. The votes must also be recorded, counted and reported honestly. The legislation should contain measures to ensure that the votes will not be tampered with between the time they are actually cast and the results are officially announced. Finally, there must be assurances that the candidates who receive the proportion of the votes required by law to be elected are effectively declared elected without delay.

The population's faith in the electoral system and its willingness to accept the results of the vote will be enhanced if the actions and decisions of election officials are subject to independent review. This will ensure that all votes properly marked and legally cast, and only those, are counted and reported. Ideally, this independent review should, under certain circumstances, be almost automatic and the costs to participants minimal, if any.

If the review has uncovered errors or unacceptable practices which may have affected the results of the democratic exercise, measures should exist in the law to remedy the situation and, if necessary, to right any wrongs.

Abstract

Paper presented by Hon C.J. Butale, MP, Botswana In his paper the author stresses that once the ballots have been cast freely, precautions should be taken to ensure that they will not be tampered with at any time. The procedure followed in Botswana for the counting of the ballots by the election officials provides for the attendance of the candidates and a few others in order to satisfy all those involved that the process is fair and honest. Requests for recounts can only be refused if, in the opinion of the returning officer, they are unreasonable.

The results in every constituency are made public as soon as counting is completed. This may vary depending on how long it takes to complete the process.

The High Court of Botswana has jurisdiction over disputed elections and, if it is satisfied that irregularities in the conduct of an election have occurred, it may void the election as it actually did in a recent instance.

Honesty in counting and announcing the votes is assured through appointment of competent and impartial election officers whose actions are subject to review by an impartial judiciary.

Discussion

In addition to the paper submitted by Mr Butale, which had been distributed in advance of the meeting, the Study Group had the benefit of two other papers on this subject, one from Mr E. E. Kazimoto, Clerk of the National Assembly of Tanzania, and the other from Dr J. W. Z. Kurewa, Secretary to the Parliament of Zimbabwe.

In answer to the question of how honesty could best be assured in the counting and announcing of votes, Mr Butale summarized his discussion paper by outlining the provisions which were in place in his country respecting the conduct of the poll and the counting and recording of votes.

The ensuing discussion then centred on a number of topics arising from the paper.

As regards the actual means of recording a vote, most Group Members reported that they used some form of ballot paper, while Botswana used a coloured paper disc system to cope with cases of illiteracy. India used a ballot paper which indicated both the candidates' names and their parties' symbols. While simple to use, the coloured disc system meant that political parties were obliged to inform the electorate about the colours used to identify them.

Respecting ballot papers, there was some discussion as to what was acceptable in terms of the type and placement of the mark used to indicate an elector's vote. It was generally agreed that a mark should be acceptable as long as it clearly indicated the intention of the voter, whether it was a cross, checkmark (tick) or other mark. The design of ballot papers was discussed and some approval was expressed for the form of the Canadian ballot.

The need for a type of 'protest' or 'declined ballot' was discussed with most delegates feeling that such a provision was not required. However, it was already provided for in one Canadian jurisdiction (Ontario) and there did seem to be some public demand for a way to express a protest vote and to have such a vote counted and reported separately from rejected or spoiled ballots. One suggestion which received some support was for provision to be made for an additional line to be included on the ballot for the voter to indicate 'none of the above' or some other indication to that effect. This would preserve the secrecy of the vote which could be endangered if the elector had to declare publicly to poll officials that he/she wished to decline the ballot paper in protest.

One jurisdiction reported on provisions that had been made to assist visually-impaired electors to mark their own ballots using a template which was placed over the ballot or notched ballots which guided electors to the name of the candidate of their choice.

Some delegates expressed concern about the safeguards which were sometimes necessary to prevent the loss of ballot boxes or the tampering with their seals between the close of the polls and the conduct of the official count. There was some indication that, if a preliminary count was conducted at the polling station immediately after the voting ended, then the effects of tampering with seals or the loss of boxes were greatly lessened, since records of the preliminary count could be used to complete the results or, alternatively, evidence could be taken from officials present at the poll when the count was made.

There was some concern expressed over the length and effects of the delay between election day and the swearing in of a new government. In fact, the delegate from New Zealand reported on a constitutional crisis which arose during the most recent change in government. One must probably conclude, however, that such delays were inherent in the parliamentary system and the particular electoral system chosen to 'translate the votes into seats'.

While the subject of voting machines was raised, it was not discussed at length, since they did not appear to be useful in majority electoral systems with single-Member constituencies.

Some discussion centred on the necessity for assuring the secrecy of the vote, with particular reference to polls where only a small number of electors were eligible to vote or which were comprised entirely of certain categories of electors (for example, the military, the police). The Study Group recommended that all possible safeguards should be built into electoral processes to assure secrecy and to prevent the identification of voting trends amongst particular categories of voters.

Conclusions

The Study Group acknowledged that, notwithstanding the social and cultural diversity of Commonwealth countries, there was great benefit to be gained from examining the electoral laws and procedures of the member countries, with a view to developing electoral systems that might better suit the needs of each. The ultimate goal, however, should always be to ensure that the principle of free and fair elections was upheld and neither eroded nor compromised.

On the question of electoral systems, the Study Group concluded that the basic principles of parliamentary democracy were still acceptable in the Commonwealth, although each country had adapted them in its own unique fashion to meet its own circumstances and societal needs, and was constantly looking for improvements. Indeed, it was stressed that the population's fundamental freedom to express its preference and elect the representatives of its choice should be more important than the system used to translate votes into seats/representation.

In redistributing electoral boundaries, equality of representation should be one of the main guiding principles. The principle of 'one vote – one value' should be uppermost, although the political, legal and institutional factors should also be taken into account.

As reported in the body of the Report, it was unanimously agreed that a recommendation should be made to the CPA that a compendium be drafted to include comparative data on the following subjects: electoral systems, constituencies, procedures, voting rights, candidates, campaigns, reporting results and judicial review.

A clear consensus emerged that in a free and democratic society opinion polls during an election should not be prohibited but regulated. In order to ensure that the polls were honest and to protect the consumer, the election legislation should contain full disclosure provisions including, for example, the name of the person or organization who commissioned the poll, its cost, the size of the sample and what was the question posed.

The Study Group also expressed the view that measures should be taken to ensure that secrecy of voting was protected in developing procedures which: (a) would permit protest votes to be cast secretly, and (b) would prevent the identification of voting trends in small polls or in recognizable groups or particular categories of electors.

Acknowledging that they had derived great benefit through learning of the procedures, on a comparative basis, in different Commonwealth countries, the Members of the Study Group expressed the wish that the officials who were responsible for the conduct of elections and the administration of election procedures in the various Commonwealth countries should collaborate with each other to: (a) exchange information, and (b) meet, whether as small groups or in plenary sessions as can be arranged, with a view to exchanging practical ideas and benefiting from the experience of others. For example, additional voting facilities were introduced in the Canadian electoral legislation to the great benefit of the Canadian electorate following firsthand observation of similar provisions in the New Zealand legislation. The experience of New Zealand in involving the postal authorities in updating the voters' lists, the use of the disc for voting in Botswana, or the role of election officials in conducting union votes in Australia, are certainly ideas which could be examined further. It was also agreed that copies of the Report of this Study Group should be distributed not only to those who normally received publications of the CPA, but specifically to the election officials in each of the Commonwealth countries.

The Study Group expressed great interest in the so called 'silent lists' in use in Australia and New Zealand to protect certain categories of voters and recommended that measures should be taken in all countries to ensure that voters' lists would not be used for purposes other than those for which they were established.

In the opinion of the Members, attempts should be made to ensure greater uniformity in the location of the polling booths for elections at the various levels of government.

During their deliberations and in the context of different questions, the Study Group insisted in a number of instances on the importance of a competent an politically neutral core of election administrators. It was recognized, however, that the problem of recruiting competent election officials was not unique to small countries. Even larger Commonwealth countries experienced, to varying degrees, similar difficulties.

Discussion of the Recommendations of the CPA Study Group

The Report of the CPA Study Group on Electoral Law and Practice was widely acclaimed by delegates participating in the conference's third plenary session.

The 9 October session was opened by Mr Patrick Boyer, MP, of Canada, who outlined the report produced by the Study Group which he chaired in Halifax, Nova Scotia, immediately before the conference. Delegates from all regions of the Commonwealth applauded the analysis of electoral systems and specifically endorsed many of the conclusions, including the proposal that the CPA should extend the Study Group's work by producing a compendium of Commonwealth electoral practices. There was also general but not unanimous support for the establishment of a Commonwealth team to monitor elections.

Divergent Views

Despite the agreement of delegates on the need for procedures which would ensure free and fair elections, there were differences of opinion on setting the voting age at 18, on restricting the publishing of opinion polls, on compulsory voting, on the use of photo-identity cards and on using factors other than population to determine constituency sizes.

An Indian delegate noted there was mounting pressure in his country for a reduction of the minimum voting age to 18 from 20. West Bengal and Barbadian colleagues also indicated support for the lower age, but a Singaporean Member questioned whether potential voters had enough education, maturity, understanding and sense of responsibility to vote at 18. He also suggested young people tended to get caught up in fads and this could lead to instability in policy matters if candidates tried to appeal to these whims. The Member also questioned the difference that existed in many states between the minimum voting age and the minimum age for citizens to stand for elections.

A United Kingdom delegate attacked the extensive use of public opinion polls in politics and especially in election campaigns. He argued the pollsters were usurping the role of Parliamentarians in determining policy and were unduly influencing election results. Publishing poll results during election campaigns could produce a bandwagon effect and alter the result of the actual vote. He suggested that opinion poll results should not be published within two weeks of voting day, a restriction in place in France. A New Zealander agreed with that proposal, while a Barbadian called for a three or four-week moratorium. But a Canadian Member expressed doubts about such a 'heavy handed' action in a free society, although he acknowledged it might be necessary.

The Canadian also had reservations about compulsory voting. He and a Malaysian state Member from Penang expressed a preference for votes cast by interested citizens, although the Canadian admitted candidates and campaigners could use their time better if they did not have to shepherd so many voters to the polls. A Maharashtra MLA countered that compulsion ensured high turnouts and prevented minorities from selecting a winner.

Members from Saint Lucia, the Malaysian state of Selangor and the Indian states of Maharashtra and West Bengal advocated the introduction of photo-identity cards to help reduce voter fraud; however, an Australian favoured the use of the cards for government programmes but not for voting.

Equality

The current Australian debate over one-vote-one-value spilled onto the conference floor. An Australian federal Member accused Queensland of gerrymandering in setting state electoral boundaries and noted that in the state of Western Australia there was up to an eleven-fold difference in the populations of some constituencies. A New Zealander termed this a breach of electoral fairness.

On the other side, a state Member from Victoria joined a federal Australian colleague in defending the allocation of more seats to large rural areas than their small populations would warrant. The needs of these rural areas had to be represented and citizens had to have reasonable access to their MPs.

Canadian, Indian and Penang delegates agreed with the concept of one-vote-one-value, but favoured a balance between demographic, geographic and other criteria in setting constituency boundaries. It was noted that one Canadian constituency spanned four time zones but had a very small population.

Mr Boyer said Canadian officials used a 25 per cent tolerance in setting constituency population sizes in order to account for other factors such as geographic area. A UK delegate maintained that urban slum dwellers could be just as isolated as people in wilderness areas, but Mr Boyer suggested that was a political problem which could not be solved by changing the voting system. Even the geographic size of a constituency was not a necessary determinant in setting boundaries since a Member's accessibility to his constituents was significantly affected by communications, transportation and other services and facilities available to him.

Electoral Challenges

The Study Group Chairman said elections were a challenge both to individual contestants and to political institutions and systems. The means of acquiring and losing power in fair, civilized and predictable ways was the basis of democracy. Electoral systems had to be both adapted to other cultures beyond the Westminster tradition, and continually modified within each country to meet changing circumstances. Members from India and Botswana were among those who agreed that voting systems could not be moved in their entirety between countries without modifications to suite local custom.

Mr Boyer was supported by Members from Trinidad & Tobago, Barbados and Saint Lucia in arguing that while election machinery must be non-partisan, there must also be some political involvement to ensure honesty by all concerned and to make use of the local expertise of MPs. In Barbados, that was done through consultation between government and opposition in selecting distinguished electoral overseers. There was also consultation in Trinidad, but impartiality was still questioned and political representation on the electoral commission was therefore said to be necessary. An Indian delegate, however, said his country's election commission was entirely non-partisan, and an Australian said politicians would manipulate the system if given a chance.

The merits of proportional representation were noted by an Australian delegate who said it was not representative for Saskatchewan's government to have 86 per cent of its Legislature seats with only 54 per cent of the popular vote, or for British minor parties to take 30 per cent of the general election vote but only seven per cent of the House of Commons seats. However, he acknowledged that proportional representation had a less successful record in producing workable government majorities. His country's preferential voting system did ensure a mathematically fair result without jeopardizing the chances of obtaining workable majorities.

Interference

The delegate from Selangor criticized the unnecessary interference by officials and the courts in the electoral process. Candidates could be removed and victories overturned on the basis of minor technicalities, thus disrupting the democratic selection of candidates.

A British MP, however, welcomed court supervision of elections to ensure fairness. Political parties and municipalities also had a supervisory role to play on voting day. The delegate endorsed the concept of a CPA supervisory team to monitor voting since free and fair elections were a hallmark of the Commonwealth which set it apart from the compulsory political system of the Soviet Union.

The United States government was attacked by a Trinidadian for propping up undemocratic regimes in the Caribbean area. While supporting a Commonwealth supervisory presence where necessary at election time, he said undemocratic regimes would not admit observers.

The Victorian Member asked for advice on an unusual situation which occurred in a recent state election. The vote had produced a dead heat and the returning officer had to cast the deciding ballot to pick a winner who would in turn decide the majority in the Legislative Council. The choice was made by drawing a name out of a ballot box, but the result was later overturned for electoral irregularities in other votes. The contest was fought again three months later under very different circumstances producing a different result. Perhaps a revote should have been held immediately instead of the casting vote being used, he suggested. A Saint Lucian Member had no objection to the casting vote, provided the returning officer did not have an original vote.

The West Bengal Member objected to what he said was the right of Indian state Governors to replace elected ministries even if the ministries had not been defeated in the House. He also supported stringent curbs on election spending so that wealthy businesses could not 'buy' elections.

New Zealand and Barbadian MPs were among those who called for more media responsibility in elections. The press should report, not influence. A Canadian criticized the media for highlighting the frivolous in campaigns rather than discussing the issues.

Other Issues

A number of delegates doubted the worth of appointed Upper Houses, and there was some support for raising the deposits and nomination requirements for candidates. The Singaporean participant in the discussion explained his country's new non-constituency Member provision and advocated the establishment of similar provisions elsewhere to ensure an opposition voice in Parliament.

Members from Botswana expressed divergent views on some matters, reflecting the multi-party character of their democracy in a region where one-party states predominated.

An Australian MP assessed electoral systems, not from an institutional perspective, but from the viewpoint of the individual voter. The rights of the individual must not be sacrificed for party political gains, he said.

Summing up the discussion, a Nova Scotia Member of the Canadian province's Legislative Assembly urged the Commonwealth Parliamentary

Association to pursue the recommendations in the Study Group Report, particularly the proposals for a compendium of Commonwealth electoral practices and a meeting of Commonwealth electoral officers. The Study Group's review of practices and the resulting conference discussion on the many variations in democratic practice had demonstrated the worth of comparing all aspects of a process fundamental to all Parliaments.

Small Countries' Views

In an earlier brief discussion of the Report at the Fifth Commonwealth Parliamentary Conference of Members from Small Countries, two particular problems related to voting in small communities were aired. A Member from the Northern Territory expressed concern about the voting assistance given to Australia's Aborigines. Those who required assistance in completing the ballot were helped by the local Australians of European descent who might well have strong political views. These people could easily influence an Aborigine's vote even though scrutineers checked to guard against that. At the very least, this violated the basic tenet of voting, the secret ballot. A Saint Lucian delegate agreed, noting that the only comparison in his community was with provisions for the blind to vote with the aid of a friend, but only the friend saw the vote.

In the Turks and Caicos Islands, residential requirements were needed to prevent the wealthy from importing the relatively small number of potential voters necessary to reverse a local result. Continuous residency was required for twelve of the 24 months before voting day. Strict spending limits were similarly required to prevent undue influence.

Index